THE LLEYN PENINSULA
COASTAL PATH

Caernarfon Castle - The castle was built at the direction of Edward I on a previously fortified site. It guards the entrance to the Menai Straits and marks the start of the walk

THE LLEYN PENINSULA COASTAL PATH

Following in the steps of the Bardsey Pilgrims

A guide for walkers and cyclists

by

JOHN CANTRELL

CICERONE PRESS
MILNTHORPE, CUMBRIA

ISBN 1 85284 252 0
A catalogue record for this book is available from the British Library

Acknowledgements

I wish to thank those who have helped me in producing this book.

Several people have walked and cycled parts of the route with me, and acted as chauffeurs. In particular I acknowledge the assistance of Heather, Wendy and Yvonne and the company of Whiskey the dog who, as usual, has walked every inch of the way even though he has now approached the grand old age of 18.

I have received much help from Arthur Rylance of Chester who has provided his skills in the darkroom to help with the photographs, and from Peter and Maureen Hunt who provided considerable encouragement.

Last, but certainly not least, I thank my parents, John (Jack) and Lee Cantrell who have been tireless in seeking out historical information from local libraries in North Wales. Without their assistance this book would never have been finished.

John Cantrell

Front Cover: The Rivals from the beach near Clynnog-Fawr

CONTENTS

List of sketchmaps

Advice to Readers

Readers are advised that whilst every effort is taken by the author to ensure the accuracy of this guidebook, changes can occur which may affect the contents. It is advisable to check locally on transport, accommodation, shops etc but even rights-of-way can be altered.

The publisher would welcome notes of any such changes

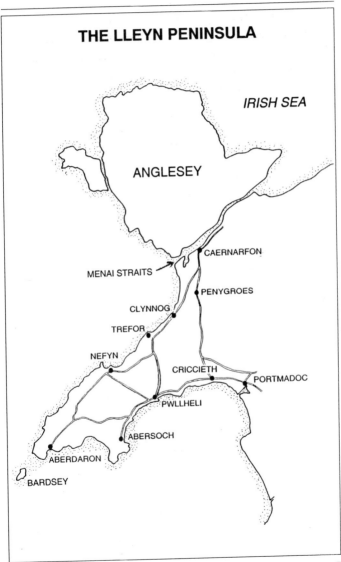

THE LLEYN PENINSULA

IRISH SEA

ANGLESEY

CAERNARFON

MENAI STRAITS

PENYGROES

CLYNNOG

TREFOR

NEFYN

CRICCIETH

PORTMADOC

PWLLHELI

ABERSOCH

ABERDARON

BARDSEY

KEY TO SKETCHMAPS

Main Route ⎯ ⎯ ⎯ ⎯ ⎯ ⎯ ⎯ ⎯

(when not on lanes, bridleways etc.)

Drystone wall

Broken wall

Hedgerow

Fence with gate

Stile A

Road

Farm track/Green lane

Bridge

Buildings

Church

Telegraph poles

Summits

Streams and rivers

Banking

Cattle grid

Steps

Trees - conifers and deciduous

Sketchmaps are numbered in line with Chapter Numbers. Thus Sketchmap 3.2 is the second map of Chapter 3, sketchmap 2.1 is the first map in Chapter 2 and so on

CHAPTER 1
Introduction

The western seaboard of England and Wales has three main peninsulas jutting out into the Atlantic Ocean and Irish Sea. Those who are old enough to remember may recall a well known national driving school using a map of the British Isles to represent a driver, Cornwall being the "leg" and the two peninsulas of Wales being the "arms" holding the steering wheel.

The most southerly peninsula is that of Devon and Cornwall, then moving north one finds the Pembrokeshire headland, and further north still is the Lleyn peninsula of North Wales. Both Devon and Cornwall, and Pembroke have justly famous coastal walks, but the Lleyn seems to have been overlooked in this regard. This is a great pity for the Lleyn has much to offer in a traverse of its coastal area.

Of course the Lleyn cannot match the sheer scale of the South-West Peninsula Coastal Path which is some 500 miles in all, nor does it even approach the Pembrokeshire Coastal Path of 170 miles. However its 90 miles contain a variety of cliff, dune, moor and mountain which is unsurpassed. Indeed its lack of miles can be seen as a positive virtue - to complete the South-West Peninsula Coastal Path in one go demands a commitment of time and effort that few people can afford. Even the Pembroke path demands a fortnight for those of normal pedestrian speeds. The Lleyn can be walked in a week without too much exertion.

In addition the Lleyn peninsula is much better defined than its two big brothers. The western end of the Menai Straits at Caernarfon obviously marks its northern limit, and Portmadoc is the finish, because to the south the coastline changes direction quite abruptly to lead into Cardigan Bay. Who can say where the South-West peninsula starts? Presumably Bristol but would Gloucester have a case? Even more confusingly, where does it end? Lyme Regis, Weymouth or even Bournemouth could make a case.

The Pembroke case is somewhat easier for it stays within the

9

county of Pembrokeshire, the county boundaries being the start and finish. However such boundaries are merely man-made limitations and the limits of the actual peninsula are more difficult to define; why should it not start at New Quay or finish at Llanelli? There are no such complications with the Lleyn peninsula; it is easily defined as everything to the west of the main A487 Caernarfon to Portmadoc road.

The Lleyn coastline has much variety. From mudflats to summits in excess of 1800ft, from sanddunes to rocky cliffs, from some of the oldest rock in the British Isles to some of the newest, and from untouched working villages to popular seaside resorts. There is also a historic precedent to walking the length of the Lleyn, for pilgrims used to make the trip in order to board a boat to Bardsey Island off the south-western tip of the Lleyn. In ecclesiastical terms, three trips to Bardsey were the equivalent of one pilgrimage to Rome.

What the Lleyn does not have is a continuous path alongside its shores and to walk the peninsula demands occasional sorties inland for a mile or two, so that existing rights of way can be used. This means ascending hills parallel with the coast, or visiting villages just inland. Nevertheless, the sea is rarely out of sight, and the majority of the walk stays close to the shoreline.

The nature of the rights of way followed by the Lleyn coastal path also allow for cyclists to enjoy many sections of the peninsula, especially on the northern side. Thus this guide acts not only for walkers but also recommends cycleways, bridleways and other byways which cyclists can legally use. The nature of some of these bridleways is often rough and steep, and is really the domain of the increasingly popular "mountain" or "all-terrain" bike.

Each section of the walk therefore deals mainly with the coastal route for walkers but also includes connections for cyclists. The historical notes and descriptions are of course equally applicable to both modes of transport.

It is recognised that not everybody wishes to complete a long distance path in one fell swoop, even one as short as the Lleyn peninsula path. Each chapter of the guide therefore ends with two or three shorter or circular walks which provide a taste of the different sections of the Lleyn, but which can be completed at one's leisure.

Gradings of Circular Walks

The circular walks are graded either A, B or C. Whilst this is very much a subjective assessment it may help when a choice has to be made.

A: Walks of a serious nature due to their distance, or height above sea level. Tracks may be indistinct or non-existent and reasonable skill with map and compass would be needed, particularly in bad weather.

B: Walks on obvious tracks or with plain landmarks. Nevertheless such walks may cross boggy or difficult ground and boots are recommended.

C: Easy walks on good tracks suitable for all ages.

Maps

The vast majority of the Lleyn coastal path is covered by the Ordnance Survey Landranger map number 123 - somewhat predictably entitled "Lleyn Peninsula". This gives a good overall impression of the walk at a scale of 1:50,000. For better detail, including field boundaries, the Ordnance Survey Pathfinder series at a scale of 1:25,000 are excellent. Appendix 1 gives the details of all such maps (7) needed to cover every inch of the route.

The sketchmaps in this book are intended to complement the OS maps. They do not cover all the route, are not exactly to scale, and do not show features such as contour lines or detail other than directly on the line of the route. Their purpose is to assist the passage in places of particular complexity such as farms and to confirm the existence of stiles, gates, walls, fences and other features not noted on OS maps.

The author is well aware that the landscape is not static or dead, and changes do occur. It is possible that what is described as a "ruin" in the book may have been renovated, and field boundaries can and do change. The aim of the maps in this book therefore is to include enough detail so that even if one or two changes occur there is still sufficient detail to follow the route with confidence.

The whole route follows footpaths, bridleways, byways and lanes. All such thoroughfares are rights of way and one has a legal entitlement to use them. Occasionally one may come across illegal blockages to rights of way, usually new fences. However, this has been found to be a very minor problem on the described route. Any such blockages have been reported to the appropriate County Highways Authorities, but if a right of way is found to be blocked it is worth forwarding a letter to the Authority. For those who wish to know more of their rights and obligations concerning such matters the Ramblers Association produces some excellent literature.

Equipment

Normally following a coastal path means that a good deal less skill is needed with map and compass than following a high traverse across desolate mountains - keep walking and keep the sea on the right might appear to be all that is needed! Unfortunately, as noted above, the Lleyn Peninsula Coastal Path does not stay at the edge of the ocean and makes occasional sorties inland. Even a cursory glance at the map shows the mountains of Yr Eifl blocking the way along the northern side of the peninsula.

Thus the path does cross higher land than is generally the case with coastal walks, and at its highest point reaches a height of 1345ft (with an optional excursion to 1670ft). One of the shorter circular walks reaches a height of 1850ft. Such stretches are not very long but the country is unpopulated and desolate. Such areas demand reasonable competence with map and compass for whilst the way is straightforward on a clear sunny day, conditions can soon change above 1000ft with mist descending and wind speed rising.

The way for cyclists does not reach such dizzy heights! Nevertheless one bridleway reaches a height of 1150ft. At this point the track is wide and well defined but it can still be decidedly chilly!

As well as map and compass the usual extras should be carried as for any day out in the country: waterproofs, warm clothing, food, whistle and torch. Walkers are recommended to wear boots as the route has its occasional boggy sections. Modern lightweight ones are ideal. Cyclists follow a slightly drier route, but there is still the odd ford or wet patch to cross. In a very dry year cyclists might risk wearing trainers or similar footwear, but lightweight boots are excellent for mountain-biking. Cyclists may also wish to wear protective headgear.

The warnings above may seem rather daunting, but are not

meant to discourage. Any reasonably fit person who walks regularly in the countryside will find this route holds no dangers and many pleasures. Even the novice walker or families should have no real difficulty if care is taken. The higher sections can be avoided, if necessary, by using lower lanes and secondary roads, but at the price of less pleasant scenery and views.

HISTORY

a) The Geology of the Lleyn

In historical terms the Lleyn can go back as far as the beginnings of time. Some of the oldest rocks in the world can be found on the peninsula. The standard table of geological time scales names the oldest rocks as Pre-Cambrian which refers to rocks over 600 million years old. Certain formations in this category reach ages of up to 2500 million years old, and such rocks can be found in the Lleyn peninsula and also in Anglesey. As one might expect there is precious little information concerning this era, but note is made in the description of the walk as to the location of some of these particularly ancient rocks. The Lleyn is generally made from old hard rocks. Even those areas not coming into the Pre-Cambrian category mostly come into the Cambrian and Ordovician categories, which are the oldest classifications after Pre-Cambrian.

The geology of Lleyn is of course closely connected with the upheavals which formed the main part of the Snowdonia National Park. The huge pressures which formed the mountains of Snowdonia also crumpled and folded the rocks of the Lleyn so that there is a great confusion of rocks. Added to this are more recent additions such as the volcanic activity of some 70 million years ago when basalt lava was forced upwards, solidifying to form hard bands called dykes.

In recent times, geologically speaking, the various Ice Ages ensured that the Lleyn was covered in ice sheets many hundreds of feet thick. These sheets scoured and eroded the rocks of the Lleyn, but as they melted and receded the material which was embedded in the ice was deposited on the landscape. This material is a mixture of pebbles, clay sand and mud which has been ground together and is called boulder clay.

The most recent geological changes to the Lleyn are the mudflats and dune areas. When the vast sheets of ice melted, the land, which had been pressed down by the huge weight of ice, tended to rise up. This is apparent from certain old beaches which are now raised above the coastline. The sea, pounding away all the while, created new beaches and sanddunes, while rivers flowing again when the ice had gone brought mud and shale down to the coast.

It is the variety of old and new, of deposits and volcanics side by side, of land movements both up and down which gives the Lleyn its rich diversity of scenery. The mixture of coastal cliff, sandy bays, moorland, heath and dune ensure that there is no chance to become bored on this route.

b) Human history

The Lleyn is well endowed with relics of history. The first settlers who left any trace of their culture were peoples of the early stone age who lived here around 8000 BC. The custom of burying their dead under stone monuments ensured that they left their mark on the landscape. Examples of their work can be found on St. Tudwal's peninsula, south of Abersoch and in the area west of Aberdaron. The south side of the peninsula was home to Neolithic settlers who had learned the art of making stone tools. The axe factory on Mynydd Rhiw is an example of their industry. However the most obvious early features are the Iron Age hill forts. Not surprisingly these are found on the summits of the volcanic outcrops such as Garn Fadryn and Garn Boduan. The best preserved of all the hill forts is on Yr Eifl and is called Tre'r Ceiri or the "Town of the Giants".

Often a trip to such sites is disappointing for the layman. Only an expert can make out the line of the fort and the remains of the various buildings supposedly associated with it. It seems that a fertile imagination is needed to "see" the ruin. This is not the case with Tre'r Ceiri. The ramparts, defences and the circular huts are all plain to see. There has been a certain amount of restoration work but even those parts which have not been restored are in a good state of preservation. The site forms the basis of one of the circular walks in Chapter 3 (see p56).

The Romans who spent a good deal of effort in subduing the Welsh tribes do not appear to have bothered too much with the

Lleyn. The defence of Wales was based on a series of forts and roads. Caernarfon was the most westerly of the major forts, and there are no important fortifications on the Lleyn; indeed there are very few Roman remains of any sort on the Lleyn. There is a small fortified outpost at Derwydd-Bach (OS Ref: 477454). This is now a reed covered site and the remains are hardly visible on the ground. In any case it is only 300 yards west of the A487 road which we have taken as the demarcation line of the peninsula. Thus it only gets on to the Lleyn by a whisker!

Dinas Dinlle (see walk (a), Chapter 2 p27) had a small Roman fortification at the southern end of the beach on the site of an earlier Iron Age fort. This was probably a signalling station for the main fort at Caernarfon. It commands an excellent view of the entrance to the Menai Straits. Finally the 6 inch OS map shows some small Roman remains at Tremadoc, including a bath house, and some sort of shrine. It is likely these remains were originally part of some larger villa.

Despite the general lack of remains the Roman influence would have been felt across the Lleyn. It is not without significance that there is a famous gravestone in the churchyard of the village of Llangian. Llangian is just inland from Hell's Mouth and therefore a considerable way down the peninsula. The grave is marked by a stone pillar with the words "Melius the Doctor, son of Martinus, lies here". The words are in Latin, confirming the Roman influence. Further details of this pillar are given in the cycling route which passes through the village.

The Anglo-Saxons appear to have taken their lead from the Romans and there is precious little of their culture to be found on the Lleyn. The Normans left the occasional relic in the form of isolated Mottes and certain roads, particularly around the Abersoch and Nefyn areas.

More important changes to the geography of the Lleyn occurred between the 13th and 17th centuries when a variety of wars and Acts of Parliament had an impact on the area. The Enclosure Acts ensured that the traditional open fields shared among a community were replaced with small holdings and enclosed pastures.

As befits a peninsula the Lleyn has always had strong links with the sea, both for trading purposes and, no doubt much to the annoyance of the inhabitants, in terms of invasions by unfriendly raiding parties. Many villages therefore grew up as fishing villages and small ports. During the 18th and 19th centuries both Nefyn and Porth Dinllaen achieved a certain reputation for shipbuilding.

The shipping trade was greatly helped by the increase in quarrying. One glance at the mountains of Yr Eifl shows the huge scars which resulted. Trefor, the village below the mountain, was a thriving port sending stone to the industrial towns of North West England. Other communities thrived briefly on the prosperity of mining, but the trade soon diminished, and derelict hamlets bear testimony to the decline.

In the 20th century there have been more foreign raiding parties, but they are now called "tourists". The impact of tourism has had its effects on the local economy, and it is necessary to manage this industry with as much vigour as any other. To this end large parts of the peninsula have been given the protection of the status of Area of Outstanding Natural Beauty, and in the 1970s over 50 miles of the coastline were designated as a Heritage Coast. Whilst there are those who say that the protection such designation gives is insufficient it is at least a recognition of the beauty of the scenery.

c) The Pilgrims Route to Bardsey

Bardsey Island is right at the tip of the peninsula. It is called in Welsh *Ynys Enlli*. For hundreds of years it was a particularly holy site and pilgrims made their way along the peninsula to reach Aberdaron from where a boat could take them the last few miles to Bardsey. Many holy stopping places developed along the peninsula to cater for both the spiritual and human needs of the pilgrims.

In following the coastal path the walker is continuing an ancient tradition, which can give as much pleasure now as it no doubt did to the early pilgrims. Three pilgrimages to Bardsey counted in ecclesiastical terms as one trip to Rome. (Some authorities say that the three trips counted as one trip to Jerusalem.) However I do not suggest that by walking the coastal path three times you can count it as the Pennine Way!

The main Pilgrims Route is along the North Coast and sites that have been identified as holy stopping places along that coast are as follows, starting from Caernarfon: Llanwnda, Llandwrog, Clynnog-fawr, Llanaelhaearn, Pystyll, Nefyn, Edern, Tudweiliog, Penllech, Llangwnnadl and Aberdaron.

The significance of many of these places is related in the text as the route reaches the appropriate point. It is interesting to note that all pilgrims follow the North Coast. One is forced to speculate that pilgrims from the south of England would reach the Lleyn first at Portmadoc. Why then did they not follow the South Coast of the Lleyn to reach Bardsey?

In fact there are ancient relics and holy sites on the South Coast and there are connections with certain of the saints of Bardsey in some of the South Coast villages. Nevertheless such sites are ignored by earlier references to the route the pilgrims took. A further question for pilgrims from the south of England and Wales is which way did they go home after reaching Bardsey?

One can speculate that the North Coast route was originally of no greater importance than the South Coast but certain very famous saints such as Bueno, of whom more later, settled on the North Coast and that became the traditional route. The completion of the whole coastal walk will ensure all possibilities are covered.

What then of Bardsey itself? It is said that 20,000 saints are buried on the island. There is a legend that the soul of anybody buried on Bardsey cannot go to Hell, which might explain its popularity as a resting place. However, before you book a plot, one interpretation of the legend is that the inhabitants of Bardsey were all so pious and Godfearing that this is the real reason why they never went to Hell.

There are many stories of Welsh, Irish and Breton saints. Some names are well known - St. Patrick and St. Columbus for instance - others less so. The thing they had in common was their travelling along the western seaboard of the British Isles and continental Europe.

Tradition states that one St. Cadfan sailing up from Brittany with a company of monks landed on Bardsey and founded an abbey. Most sources put this event in the first half of the 6th century, but one or two place it earlier. The level of influence of a particular saint can be gauged by the number of dedications to him (or his followers) in the names of holy sites and ancient churches. Using this method St. Cadfan's influence can be traced from the Gower in

South Wales to Anglesey. Thus it is by no means improbable that he could have visited Bardsey, but his name is not found there.

Cadfan's successor as the Abbot of the Abbey is said to be St. Lleuddad. His influence is found in connection with Bardsey where there is a field bearing his name. In addition the church at Aberdaron is jointly dedicated to him. Another of Cadfan's followers, St. Maelrhys, has a church dedicated to him between Aberdaron and Rhiw.

The question is whether St. Cadfan was the first holy man of Bardsey or whether there had been monks and hermits on the island at an even earlier date. What little evidence there is suggests that holy men were using Bardsey before the year 500 AD. This would predate most estimates of Cadfan's arrival. A sliver of evidence comes from the life of St. Dyfrig, who is confirmed as a mature man of the church in 521 AD for he was by then a full bishop.

Towards the end of his life he retired to Bardsey and died there. His name is not mentioned in the lists of those associated with Cadfan yet he was famous in his own right. It seems likely that he predated Cadfan. Such other evidence as there is also points to the fact that there were holy men on Bardsey before Cadfan's arrival.

The monks of Bardsey had a difficult life, not only in sustaining themselves through farming and fishing, but in dealing with pirates and raiders. The community managed to prosper over the centuries but not without many upsets. Those wishing to delve more deeply into this fascinating subject should consult the bibliography for further reading.

In 1979 the ownership of the island passed to the Bardsey Island Trust and it was declared a National Nature Reserve in 1986. The island is particularly famous for its birdlife, resident and migratory. An observatory was established in 1953 and involves itself in the ringing and subsequent tracking of birds.

CHAPTER 2

Caernarfon to Penygroes

CAERNARFON - The Start

Caernarfon lies on the site of an ancient settlement going back beyond Roman times. Its position at the southern end of the Menai Straits and the port facilities offered by the mouth of the Afon Seiont make it an obvious site for a settlement.

The Romans established their fort, named Segontium, on a small hillock overlooking the present town. It is in an excellent state of preservation and is well worth a visit. Take the Beddgelert road out of the town and the fort is soon seen on the left. When the Roman empire fell a small settlement remained near to the Roman camp as witnessed by the site of the parish church which is next to the Roman fort. The church is dedicated to St. Peblig.

The Menai Straits and Caernarfon Castle.
The walk starts along the shores of the straits

St. Peblig appears to predate the Bardsey saints, being the offspring of Macsen Wledig, a Roman Emperor who took a wife from these parts during the Roman occupation. The wife was called Helen and gave her name to the Roman road which runs from Conwy right through Wales to Carmarthen. The trackway is still referred to as the 'Sarn Helen'.

Caernarfon is more famous for another defensive site, the castle of Edward I which dominates the main square, innovatively named Castle Square! This is one of the series of castles built or enlarged by Edward I to pacify the Welsh, and is in the curtain wall style. Defensive town walls radiated from the castle and enclosed the area occupied today by Church Street, Market Street and High Street.

Building of the castle started some-time around 1283, when an earlier construction built by the Norman nobleman Hugh d'Arranches was enlarged and improved. By this date the Pilgrims Route to Bardsey was well established. Eight hundred years ago travellers stood by this very same castle ready to start the walk along the Lleyn.

Since the early 14th century the various Princes of Wales have been invested at Caernarfon. The latest was Prince Charles who was invested as the 21st Prince of Wales on 1st July 1969.

The other notable person having connections with Caernarfon was David Lloyd George who was the MP for the constituency for several years. He lived near Criccieth, and so, near the end of the circuit of the peninsula, Lloyd George will feature again. There is a statue of him in Castle Square.

On the west side of the castle is the harbour. The large car park was once the main loading area for a lucrative trade in slate. This was quarried just a few miles inland to the south, and then exported via Caernarfon. Nowadays the only boats in this harbour are pleasure boats and yachts, with a few working fishing boats.

There is therefore much of interest to see in Caernarfon. The sites of interest are all well documented and further information can be obtained from the tourist office.

The route starts by the castle walls close by the harbour. Here there is a footbridge, known as the Aber bridge, which leads over the mouth of the Afon Seiont to the other side of the harbour. The bridge

Caernarfon towards Saron

Sketchmap 2.1

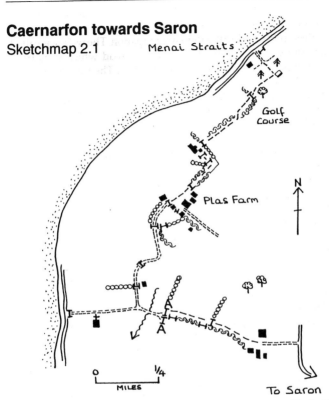

Menai Straits

Golf Course

Plas Farm

N

0   ¼

MILES

To Saron

is closed between 11pm and 7am each day, but it seems unlikely that many people would wish to start the walk during these hours.

Once over the bridge turn right (NW) and follow the little lane alongside the water. There are excellent views across the Menai Straits to the Anglesey coast on the opposite side. The straits are only about a mile wide here, but are well respected for there are dangerous currents and swift tidal flows which make the waters hazardous.

There is a wide variety of seabirds to observe over the water and scavenging in the sand and mud banks at the side of the straits. The remains of a "swimming baths" is soon passed on the right. This was a simple affair with a retaining wall and a basin which filled naturally with sea water. It does not look very inviting!

After walking along the pleasant lane for about a mile a golf club appears on the left (OS Ref: 464622). Just before the entrance to the club a footpath sign points through a swing gate and a faint track leads through to the car park - sketchmap 2.1. Directly behind the car park (S) the land rises up a grassy slope, climb this to arrive at a tee with good views across the golf course. Walk down off the tee trending right (SSW) to a hedgeline and a tree. A gate will be found in the undergrowth.

Pass through the gate and follow the slightly curving hedgeline to a gap in the hedge. Pass through the gap but stay by the line of the hedge, which is now on the right. Soon a wall is reached with an obvious gate. Leave the golf course by the gate then turn sharp left (SE) in front of the buildings whence two further gates give access to a green lane. Turn right (SSW) along the lane to arrive at Plas Farm (OS Ref: 463613).

The route through the farm is a little complex. Pass the two new barns on the left, and then the farmhouse also on the left. The right of way should go left straight after the farmhouse onto the farm lane. After 50 yards or so a turn should then be made into the field on the right, to pass the side of the very old barns. However the access into this field is difficult as there is no trace of a stile or gate.

An easy alternative presents itself. Instead of turning left round the farmhouse and along the farm lane, bear slightly right at the farmhouse and through a gate between two of the old barns. This leads you along an obvious track to a point (50 yards) where there are two gates side by side. Take the right-hand gate and follow the obvious track past the barn at Ysgubor Fawr (OS Ref: 458609) to reach a track junction from where a small church can be seen on the right (W) some 200 yards away.

This is the ancient church of St. Baglan, the church now being known as Llanfaglan church. It is well worth making a visit. It was renovated in 1993 but it is difficult to see where the congregation comes from, as, apart from a couple of isolated farms, there is no centre of population nearby.

There seems to be little information on who St. Baglan was or what his claim to fame might be. The only reference to the church in the Caernarfon archives office is from an article in the newspaper *The Caernarfon and Denbigh Herald* of 31st August 1934.

The article notes that this is one of the smallest and oldest churches in North Wales. There is evidence of a church on the site some 700 years ago. This would be somewhat late for Bardsey pilgrims but such ancient sites were often built on the site of an even older holy place. Part of the difficulty with St. Baglan is that there appear to have been two saints of the same name. One of them was the brother of Lleuddad, who was the second abbot of Bardsey and if the church is named after this particular Baglan then a pilgrims connection seems probable.

The porch to the church is a later addition but on the land side is an oblong aperture in the wall, the lintel and sill of which are ancient coffin stones. These were reputedly dug up nearby. The slight taper of the line of the coffin can be seen, and it is noteworthy that each has a large Celtic cross engraved upon it. Taking all the available evidence it seems likely that the site is an ancient one, and may well have been visited by the early Bardsey pilgrims. Retrace your steps to reach the track junction.

For those without the time to visit the church a left turn is made (WSW) over a little stream to reach a triple set of gates with stiles to the right and left. Pass over the left-hand stile. Walk along the edge of the field following the hedgeline. Soon two gates are reached, the one to the right being ignored as the route carries straight on. The track becomes shale and barns appear on the right and a farmhouse on the left. Pass between the house and barns to walk along the farm lane which soon develops a tarmac surface.

A 'T' junction is reached after 300 yards (OS Ref: 465605). Turn right along the narrow lane, which swings sharply to the left. The lane soon starts to veer to the right and as it straightens a good lookout should be kept on the right for a gate with a stone stile, which is somewhat overgrown. A telegraph pole in the field provides a helpful clue. Clamber over the stone stile and follow the fenceline across the field to a gate. Pass through and keep in the same direction to another gate by a house called Freeholder (OS Ref: 467602). Walk past the house and down the access lane to a road. Turn right (SW) along the road.

Soon the house of Caer Efail is seen on the right, with its large gates. A few yards past the gates the road bends to the right, and at this point there is a stile on the left. Go over the stile and walk along the hedgeline over a further stile to arrive at a gate and road. Turn right along the road. Stay on this road which drops to the bridge over the Afon Gwyrfai to climb towards the little village of Saron.

Soon the village of Saron is reached and a row of houses appears on the right. On the left-hand side of the road is a telephone box (OS Ref: 465591), and just before the telephone box is a footpath sign and a clear track leading off to the left (E). See sketchmap 2.2. Go through the gate to the end of a short green lane and then through a further gate. Bear slightly left and follow the wall until a wall across the line forces a change of direction. Turn right to reach a solitary oak tree. At the oak tree keep left into a small enclosure with two gates. Pass through the right-hand gate.

Walk alongside the wall on a faint track to reach a stile. Over the stile stay in the same direction keeping to the middle of the meadow to reach the hedgeline on the hillside above. There is a stile in the hedge but it is not easy to see until close to it, and it may be necessary to search around. Over the stile go directly up the steeper meadow trending slightly left (ESE) to a

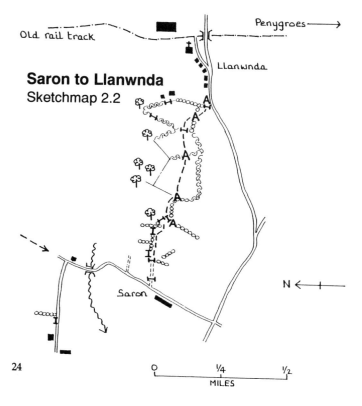

Old rail track

Penygroes

Llanwnda

Saron to Llanwnda
Sketchmap 2.2

Saron

N

0   ¼   ½
MILES

gate. Through the gate keep right by a wall. In 100 yards a stile crosses the wall where houses and a gate can plainly be seen to the left. The path emerges onto a lane by a footpath sign (OS Ref: 474586). Turn left (E).

Walk along the lane for 120 yards, and where the lane starts to rise over a bridge a narrower lane forks off to the left. Follow the narrower lane, which is signposted to a cycleway (Lon Eifion), past houses and a church to a disused railway track (OS Ref: 476586). This is the village of Llanwnda, the first on the list of stopping places for Bardsey pilgrims as noted in Chapter 1.

The church is the parish church and is dedicated to St. Gwyndaf Hen. Gwyndaf Hen plays an important role in the families of saints connected with the Lleyn. He had connections with King Arthur, as will be seen later in the walk, but he was the son of Emyr Llydaw, who was a minor royal from Brittany. Emyr Llydaw together with Einion, the supposed "king" of the Lleyn at the time, are said to have established a small monastery on Bardsey. This would conflict with the commonly held view that St. Cadfan was the first to develop Bardsey as a holy place.

Einion is remembered in the church at Llanengan, on the South Coast of the Lleyn near Abersoch. The village of Llanengan is not on the walkers' route, so a diversion is necessary to visit the site. Cyclists however pass right through the village. Einion was a direct descendent of Cunedda Wledig, who founded the kingdom of Gwynedd after the fall of the Roman empire in the early 5th century.

The present church was completed in 1848, but it is on the site of a much earlier shrine. As has been noted in Chapter 1, Llanwnda was the first of the holy sites which were visited by the pilgrims en route to Bardsey. It seems then that this church marks the pilgrims' stopping place.

A look at the OS map shows that this point is some 3 miles inland from the sea, which may seem rather strange for a "coastal" walk, but at least it is in accord with the route taken by the pilgrims.

The reason why the route keeps inland at this point is easy to see from the OS map. There may be some readers who express surprise that a walk purporting to follow the Lleyn coast did not pass through the resort of Dinas Dinlle (OS Ref: 435566) as a matter of course. Dinas Dinlle is the nearest reasonable beach to Caernarfon, and marks the point where the peninsula turns to face the open sea rather than the Menai Straits.

Although it is possible to get from Caernarfon to Dinas Dinlle on rights of way, there is a complete lack of such paths to the south of the resort. Circular walk (a), at the end of this chapter, explores the area around Dinas Dinlle. Those who have the time and inclination to do this circular will see that it is unlikely that pilgrims would have stayed hard by the coast. There is ample opportunity to view the mudflats and swamps which would have made travel in the 6th century even harder than it is today. The pilgrims kept some way inland visiting the holy site at Llanwnda.

A disused railway has been converted into a walking and cycling route by removal of the rails and smoothing of the surface. This is a good initiative and one wonders why the practice has not been followed in more areas of the country as railways have closed. This particular track runs from Caernarfon to Pwllheli on the south side of the Lleyn. The Lleyn coastal path does not stay with it for long because it cuts inland, but for the next $3^{1}/2$ miles the walking is easy and the navigation even easier!

Walk to the railway track where the main route turns right (S). Soon the busy A499 road is reached. Take care in crossing to reach the relative tranquillity of the railway bed on the opposite side. At this point is the Goat Inn, the first place on the walk where refreshment and food can be obtained.

Continue along the railway for just under 3 miles to reach the large village of Penygroes. The village marks the end of the first section of the walk. Despite its size Penygroes is not a tourist centre, and accommodation is not as easy to find as you might expect. There are virtually no bed and breakfast establishments. It is not normally the author's aim to advertise, but the scarcity of lodgings means that at least one suggestion must be made. This is Mrs Humphreys of Bryn Awel in Water Street who provides bed and breakfast. (Tel: 01286 881 283). There are two buildings which sport the sign "Hotel", but which are in fact only pubs. There is a reasonable variety of shops, pubs and a post office.

CYCLISTS

The section from Caernarfon is not well endowed with bridleways or other tracks which cyclists may legally use. However the lanes and byways in the area attract very little traffic and are pleasant enough.

Start at the same point as the walkers by Caernarfon castle, and cross the Aber bridge. Cycle along the coast road passing the "swimming pool". The golf club soon appears on the left, the point at which the walkers set off across country. Cyclists must stay on the coast road. Just over a mile after the golf club the sign to St. Baglan's church is seen. The site is described in the walkers' route above.

Keep on the lane by the sea until a sharp turn to the left (E) takes the road inland. Keep straight on ignoring a minor turn on the left to reach a 'T' junction. Walkers and cyclists are together at this point. Turn right and follow the road to reach the telephone box at Saron (OS Ref: 464591). This is the point at which the walkers cut off once again across the fields.

From the telephone box at Saron cycle straight on (SW) and take the first turn left. Follow this to a 'Y' junction by a country school and take the left-hand branch of the 'Y' to reach the point where the walkers emerge onto the lane just prior to the disused railway (OS Ref: 475586). Turn onto the railway bed, which has been specifically designed as a cycle route. It is now an easy ride south on a good hardcore surface to reach the village of Penygroes.

Alternative for Cyclists

For those who dislike tarmac it is possible to join the disused railway in Caernarfon itself. This provides a pleasant and traffic free environment all the way to Penygroes. The drawback is that the coastal views across the Menai Straits are missed.

The start of the cycleway is 250 yards south-west of Caernarfon castle. From the river by the castle do NOT cross the Aber bridge but cycle across the car park by the quayside to reach a small industrial area. The start of the cycleway is on the left, served by a car park.

OTHER WALKS IN THIS AREA
a) Dinas Dinlle Circular

Start:	On the promenade, in the village
Car park:	Ample parking on the promenade, bus service from Caernarfon
OS Ref:	436566
Distance:	6 miles

Ascent:	Virtually nil
Grade:	B (several wet sections)

It has been noted in the description of the main route that pilgrims avoided Dinas Dinlle, the nature of the terrain and the existence of the church in Llanwnda being the reasons. However, the resort is worth a visit on several counts. There are a couple of interesting historical landmarks; there are excellent views of the bay to the south with the mountains of Yr Eifl as a backdrop; and for the naturalist there are extensive areas of mudflats and dunes with associated wildlife. On the minus side the beach earned some notoriety in 1993 for being one of the top ten dirty beaches (it was 5th) in the country. The moral is, if you picnic here dispose of your litter properly. Happily no other beach on the Lleyn featured in the list.

Some may find Caernarfon Airport an attraction, others a noisy distraction. It is not quite on the same level as Heathrow, nor as busy, being confined to light aircraft, but those who wish can book a pleasure flight from here over the Snowdonia mountains. There is also a small museum.

Start the walk where the road arrives at the seaside and so becomes the promenade. Walk NNE for 150 yards and then turn right along a road which leads to the caravan site. The site is soon reached on the left, but stay on the lane until it degenerates into a track with a ditch on either side. Pass over a bridge and into a green lane leading to a farm. Cross the farmyard and walk down the farm road to reach a public road with a footpath sign (OS Ref: 454568). Turn left (N).

Looking straight ahead across the field a row of cottages is seen. These are old almshouses. The walk continues along the road until at OS Ref: 453574 a left turn is made into a lane leading to a house. Ignore the house and passing by it make for a ruined building whence two gates give access to a water meadow with a bridge over the river. Follow the track which soon comes alongside the river and follows its course.

Soon two stiles and gates are met at a crossroads. Keep straight on, keeping by the riverside. The track is now very obvious as it lies on top of a dyke, and soon the open expanse of the waters of Fford

Bay appear. The way now seems clear but after a mile or so the track finishes at a fence. There are dire warnings about private land! This is a little frustrating because the objective of Belan Fort is now in view and the stretch of private land is only 100 yards wide.

To comply with the dire warnings it is necessary to turn right along the fence and walk along the sea shore. Soon the fence turns inland and a left turn to follow its line soon leads to a disused road. Turn right along the road until it splits. At this point turn left and walk across the dunes keeping the main wall of Fort Belan on the right, and so reach the causeway leading to the main gate. A detour to visit the fort can be made from this point. If such a visit is not to be made go across the causeway, and following a line of white posts climb up onto the line of dunes ahead when the open sea comes into view. Turn left and follow any of the many tracks through the dunes to pass the airport and so arrive back on the promenade.

Although a somewhat forgotten resort these days Dinas Dinlle has some claims to fame. The hill at the south-west end of the promenade was used by the Romans as a minor fort and lookout station. Coins dated 293 AD have been found on the site from the reign of Emperor Alectus.

No Welsh village is really complete without a legend, and Dinas Dinlle has one which earns a mention in that most ancient of collections of Welsh stories, the *Mabinogen*. The story goes that one Ariaurhod, who was the mother of Lleu, cursed her son by refusing to give him a name or arm him with weapons. This was apparently a major disgrace at the time in question and left the victim without power. Gwydion, a magician, wanted to help Lleu and came to visit him at Ariaurhod's castle, situated at Dinas Dinlle. Gwydion tricked Ariaurhod into naming her son, which restored his powers. Later Ariaurhod's castle (Caer Ariaurhod) was engulfed by a huge wave and slipped into the sea.

There are a number of Welsh legends of villages and castles disappearing beneath the waves, and this may be a folk memory of a calamity in AD 331 when freak waves are said to have drowned several areas of coastal flats. When the tide is low at Dinas Dinlle stones can be seen jutting out of the sea. These are reputed to be the remains of Caer Ariaurhod.

More recently, in the 18th century a Spanish galleon under full sail was lost off the bay when it sank after going aground. As in all good tales it was reputed to be carrying treasure, but exactly what type of treasure remains a mystery. Spanish coins were regularly washed up on the beach, but none has been found in recent years. The cannons from the wreck are now at Fort Belan.

b) South Caernarfon Circular

Start:	Caernarfon Castle
Car park:	Ample in Caernarfon
OS Ref:	477626
Distance:	7 miles
Ascent:	175ft
Grade:	C

A short but pleasant excursion following the main route for a while and returning on the disused railway. Start by the castle and cross the little bridge. Now follow instructions as for the start of the main walk until the disused railway line is reached. Instead of turning right to follow the main route turn left and follow the disused railway back into Caernarfon, passing through some fine woods. The railway ends in the old goods yard but continuing in the same direction on the road leads back to the castle in 250 yards.

CHAPTER 3
Penygroes to Nefyn

This is a long section of the walk and contains all the hill walking, including the highest point traversed by the route as it crosses the line of the Rival mountains. Once Nefyn is reached the walking stays, for a considerable distance, close by the sea shore, and is of a different character to this section.

That is not to say that the whole distance between Penygroes and Nefyn must be done in one day for there are accommodation possibilities at both Clynnog-fawr and Trefor. In fact the main route by-passes Clynnog in the interests of scenic grandeur, but for those with enough time, a short diversion to Clynnog is recommended because it was one of the major holy sites on the Pilgrims Route. Cyclists, prevented from crossing the main hills near Clynnog (legally only a right of access on foot), visit Clynnog as part of their route.

The Lon Eifion cycleway - the lay-by marks the point, described in the text, where the route leaves the cycleway

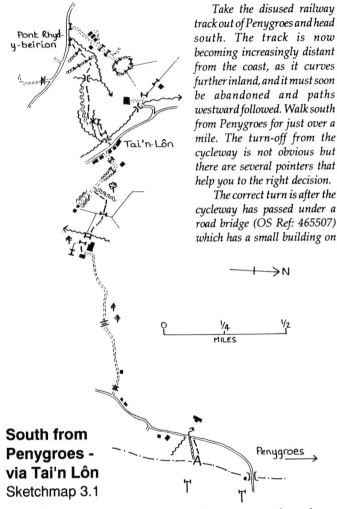

Take the disused railway track out of Penygroes and head south. The track is now becoming increasingly distant from the coast, as it curves further inland, and it must soon be abandoned and paths westward followed. Walk south from Penygroes for just over a mile. The turn-off from the cycleway is not obvious but there are several pointers that help you to the right decision.

The correct turn is after the cycleway has passed under a road bridge (OS Ref: 465507) which has a small building on

South from Penygroes - via Tai'n Lôn
Sketchmap 3.1

its south side. The building appears to have been some sort of store for use with the railway. Shortly after the bridge there are two iron blocks either side of the trackway that narrow it. Their purpose is unclear but they are

The northern Lleyn coast
Views over Trefor from Gyrn Goch

obvious. Keep an eye to the left (E) now and note a stile, and electric pylons. The trackway then widens on the left almost like a lay-by (see photograph). At this point climb the bank to the right (W) to reach the fence and maybe a stile. (For reasons that remain obscure, it has recently been removed into the field nearby.) See sketchmap 3.1.

Walk 100 yards down the meadow to the point where a stream meets the lane and turn left (SW) along the lane. In 200 yards there is a turning on the left which is ignored and in a further ¼ mile an obvious unmade track appears on the right (OS Ref: 458501). Take this track which climbs gently up the hillside. Keep on the track to a high point by a small plantation of conifers, then drop down into a farmyard at Erw-wen (OS Ref: 450498).

Pass in front of the farmhouse, then turn right below the barn (NW) and pass through two gates into a meadow with a fence on the left. Continue in the same direction along the fence to pass through a further gate leading onto open hillside with gorse bushes above to the right. Walk for 75 yards to an old hedgeline leading downhill. There is a spring at the top end of the hedge. Turn left and walk downhill alongside the hedge to reach a green lane. This lane served a ruined farmhouse in times past. Turn right (NW) down the lane to a gate by some more ruins. Through the gate turn sharp left (SW) to reach a road and footpath sign.

(If walking the coastal path in the opposite direction take care when leaving the green lane for the open hillside. If the ruins of the old farm are reached retrace your steps for 100 yards - sketchmap 3.1.)

Turn right along the road passing through the hamlet of Tai'n-lôn. Stay on the road for only 100 yards until a footpath sign is seen on the left, opposite a long low cottage. This is where walkers and cyclists must part company temporarily.

At the footpath sign by the low cottage, walkers should turn left along the footpath and over the stream to a small gate - sketchmap 3.1. Through the gate follow the fenceline as it curves round to the right until another gate is reached on the left. Pass through and over another stream and along the line of a hedge which curves again to the right until it reaches a stream by some trees. A slab bridge leads over the stream and into a poor meadow with reeds and gorse. Ahead can be seen a stone wall in which there are two gates, the right of way passing through the right-hand gate which is less

The cursed village in Nant Gwrtheyrn

The approach to Bwlch Mawr
Sketchmap 3.2

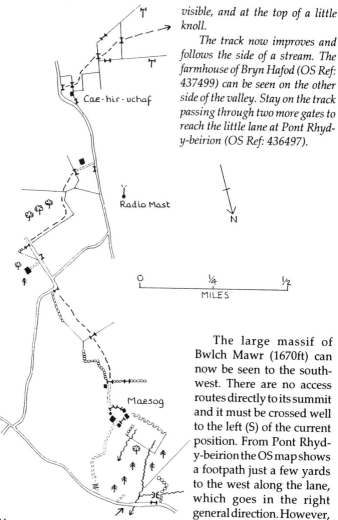

visible, and at the top of a little knoll.

The track now improves and follows the side of a stream. The farmhouse of Bryn Hafod (OS Ref: 437499) can be seen on the other side of the valley. Stay on the track passing through two more gates to reach the little lane at Pont Rhyd-y-beirion (OS Ref: 436497).

The large massif of Bwlch Mawr (1670ft) can now be seen to the south-west. There are no access routes directly to its summit and it must be crossed well to the left (S) of the current position. From Pont Rhyd-y-beirion the OS map shows a footpath just a few yards to the west along the lane, which goes in the right general direction. However,

Bwlch Mawr

Cae·hir·uchaf

The climb onto Bwlch Mawr.
The route hereabouts looks confusing but in fact all the gates are obvious and
progress is straightforward. The views over Snowdonia as height is gained are
excellent and from an unusual angle

although one can find traces of old gateways indicating that the route was well used in the past, the creation of a forestry plantation and new fences has made the going difficult.

An easier way is to turn left (SE) along the lane from Pont Rhyd-y-beirion and walk for 300 yards to the concrete drive leading to the farm at Maesog (OS Ref: 438492), on sketchmap 3.2. On reaching the farmhouse turn left (SE) and walk alongside the left-hand barn to pass through the left-hand of two gates into a sunken green lane. Follow this track past a ruined barn and through three more gates to emerge at a dogleg in a lane. Keep straight on for 50 yards to a road junction (OS Ref: 443484). Keep straight on (SE) passing a farm entrance on the left and a gate on the right to reach a fence on a bank running away from the lane on the right (SW).

Climb up from the lane and over the fence and follow alongside it on its south side. Pass a bank in the field but continue by the fence until no further progress can be made due to a cross fence. Turn left (SE) and follow this fence and a small stream to a 'Y' shaped fence junction with gorse to the right. Cross the fence and walk through the gorse to a gate, whence a track leads gently uphill past some ruins (OS Ref: 438477) to a road (see photograph). The gate allowing access to the road is offset from the track about 30 yards to the right.

The next section of walking is a delight, but, being only a footpath, is denied to the cyclists. The hills of Bwlch Mawr (1670ft), Gyrn Goch (1625ft), and Gyrn Ddu (1712ft) form a wild and totally unspoilt landscape which will surprise those who thought the Lleyn was essentially a flat area. There are glorious views in all directions and the section is highly recommended.

The only drawback in following this route is that the village of Clynnog-fawr is missed. Those following the route by cycle are forced into Clynnog but this has its compensations, for the village is of great significance in plotting the Pilgrims Route to Bardsey. Any walkers who have the time or need accommodation might

The Pilgrim Stone is in the chapel of Clynnog church. The indented cross was reputedly formed by the thumb of St. Beuno!

wish to divert the 2 miles down to Clynnog.

Clynnog is apparently just a small Welsh coastal village without any great pretensions. There are shops and various types of accommodation here for the weary traveller. Despite its lack of obvious interest this is in fact a place of historic significance, a clue to which is given by the large church by the main road. The present building dates from the 16th century (restored in 1858) but it is connected to the chapel of St. Beuno which dates from around 620 AD. This chapel, a holy well nearby and the influence of St. Beuno made Clynnog one of the most important stopping places on the Pilgrims Route to Bardsey. The water from the well was supposed to have healing qualities and it was said in the 18th century that scrapings from the pillar of the chapel, dissolved in water, were good as an eyewash.

Oddly enough, this is not the only record of St. Beuno being connected with healing waters for he is closely connected with the legend of St. Winifred and the well named after her near the town of Holywell. The story states that Winifred was the daughter of a rich nobleman who placed her, whilst still young, under the care of St. Bueno who in fact was her uncle. Bueno started a small convent and Winifred together with just a few others settled there. Some time later Caradoc, a Prince of Wales, saw Winifred and was overcome by her great beauty, but as it was impossible to marry her he tried to carry her off by force. Winifred was unimpressed by the prince and fled, and he in a jealous rage raced after her and sliced off her head with a sabre, which seems rather a strange way of professing his ardour.

The severed head then rolled down the hill, through the church doors and came to rest at the side of the altar, where Bueno was conducting a service. Where the head came to rest a huge spring burst forth. What Bueno thought of all this is not recorded, but he must have had remarkable self control for he picked up the head and reunited it with the body and then by a miracle the lovely Winifred was brought back to life. Thus there was a happy ending. St. Winifred's well is also supposed to have healing powers, and in fact there is a further well named after her at Woolston (between Oswestry and Shrewsbury), the waters of which were said to be good for sore eyes. It would seem then that between them Winifred and Bueno could be the patron saints of opticians.

*To continue the walk from the point on the mountain road turn left (S)
along the road for about 400 yards to a point where the road bends left then
right at the abandoned farm of Cae-hir-uchaf (OS Ref: 437474). Walk
round the bends and past the old house, then take a gate on the right giving
access to the hillside. See sketchmap 3.2. Level with the back of the old house
pass through another gate and then bear left (SW) across the hillside but
staying close to the fence to reach a further gate. This gives access to an
enclosed field with further gates. The correct exit is via the gate directly
opposite up the hill (WSW) from where you pass under a set of telephone
wires.*

*The way continues steeply up the hillside. Above and somewhat to the
right (WNW) are two slabby outcrops of rock and the route aims to pass
just below them. In misty weather it would be necessary to take a compass
bearing. As the land begins to level out a drystone wall appears across the
line of the very faint track. There appears to be no gate or stile in the wall*

*Once the shoulder of Bwlch Mawr is attained the view opens up to the south-
west. The main route is shown but an optional climb to the summit of Gyrn Ddu
adds only about 40 minutes*

Crossing of Bwlch Mawr
and descent to Trefor
Sketchmap 3.3

A 499

*but by keeping to the right-hand end (NW)
of the wall a set of pens will be found which
allow access to the open moor beyond.*

At this point take a moment to look
back at the view to the east, for the
mountains of Snowdonia are
particularly well seen from here, and it
is an unusual viewpoint. You may also
take the moment to recover
from the steep ascent by the
pretence of admiring the view!

*Continue in much the same
direction (WSW) and soon another drystone
wall comes into view. This is a particularly
solid wall, and there is no trace of a gap or*

Gyrn Ddu
△

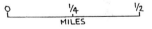

Gyrn Goch △

MILES

0   1/4   1/2

⊢———→N

stile of any sort at the place indicated on the map. A slight detour solves the problem. Walk until the wall is reached then turn right (N) and follow the wall until it turns abruptly left (W). At this point you have the option of continuing northwards and visiting the summit of Bwlch Mawr at a height of 1670ft (OS Ref: 427478), an extension which is highly recommended for its views to the south-west along the Lleyn peninsula.

Returning to the left turn in the wall, continue to follow the wall to the west until it ends in a wide gully full of boulders. Do not cross the boulder maze but turn sharp left (S) until clear of the boulders and then trend right (SW) to reach an obvious gate in the next wall. This gate is in the correct place on the right of way as shown on the OS map (OS Ref: 425467).

Pass through the gate and continue in a generally westerly direction, parallel to a wall some 100 yards away on the left. In front are good views of the two summits of Gyrn Ddu, 1712ft and Gyrn Goch, 1614ft (see photograph p38). Soon a track develops and drops between two stone walls to a gate - sketchmap 3.3. Continue in the same line, contouring round the southern slopes of Gyrn Ddu. The track improves and develops into a green lane. Several gates are passed through along with two abandoned farmhouses, Fron-heulog and Pen-y-bwlch (OS Ref: 395463). The sketchmap 3.3 covering this section is drawn at an extra large scale to facilitate navigation through the many walls and pens in this area, but the track is generally plain.

Shortly after passing the derelict farm at Pen-y-bwlch a gate in a wall gives access to a good trackway dropping down the hill in a series of sweeping bends. From this point also is the first sight of Trefor, and its harbour wall. Follow the trackway first left then swinging right below a ruined house. The purpose of the trackway soon becomes clear as old quarry workings come into view. There is soon an "S" bend with a building at its apex, and shortly after completing the "S" a left turn should be made downhill along a fainter track. There is a large square concrete foundation which points the way.

Drop down past the foundation to a level meadow at the bottom of the hill where there is a drystone wall. Turn left (W) alongside the wall until a gate appears on the right, just after a corrugated iron garage. Go through the gate and walk along the boundary of the house called Rock Cottage until a gate appears on the left. Go through the gate and straight across the lane which is the access for the house. A combined, somewhat broken, wall and fence soon appears and a gate allows further progress. Keep in the same

The Trefor area and approach to Yr Eifl
Sketchmap 3.4

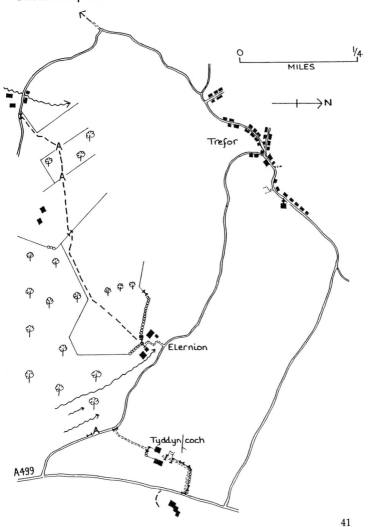

41

direction (SW) and walk into the funnel made by the narrowing of the drystone walls, and past a telegraph pole.

Follow the line of the wall but at an opening cut through to the right and then pass through the wall to find a gate at the rear of the house at Tai Newyddion (OS Ref: 384465). The gate seems to lead into the back garden of the house but it is in fact the right of way, so pass through then curve round to the left to walk to the main road at the front of the house.

Turn right (NNE) and walk along the road for 50 yards (sketchmap 3.4) when a farm track opens up on the left signed to Tyddyn-coch. Go through the gate and along the obvious farm track which soon bends to the left to pass between the barns and the farmhouse. The farm track continues (SSW) until it arrives at the road leading into Trefor (OS Ref: 382463).

The village of Trefor appears to have no historical significance relating to the Bardsey pilgrims. The area grew prosperous as a result of the mining of stone from the quarries hereabouts, but that trade has largely finished. It is a big village and although it is not on the normal tourist routes it provides accommodation and shops.

The Bardsey pilgrims visited the village of Llanaelhaearn, 2 miles south-east of Trefor. Llanaelhaearn was one of the main holy sites on the Pilgrims Route. In the churchyard there is a stone pillar with a Latin inscription dating from the late 5th century. There is also a stone inside the church, again with a Latin inscription which says, "Aliortus the Elmetian lies here". Elmet was a region of Britain corresponding to parts of South and West Yorkshire and it seems that Aliortus moved into Wales and died there some time in the early 6th century.

At this point there is a choice of routes. The next objective is the farm at Elernion (OS Ref: 378464). This can be reached by turning left (S) along the road and after 100 yards taking a stile on the right. Here there is a sign explaining that you are in Coed Elernion, a small area of woodland owned by the Woodland Trust. There is a board showing footpaths which can be followed to the farm at Elernion, but take care as once in the woods the footpaths are a little confusing.

Less pleasant, but navigationally easier, is to turn right (NW) at the road and walk along it until the farm lane to Elernion opens up on the left. Walk down the farm lane and keep on the lane to the left of the main farmhouse. Here will be found two gates, and the way lies through the upper right-hand gate. (Those who have walked through the woods of Coed

Elernion will arrive at this point via the lower left-hand gate.)

Once through the gate strike diagonally across (SW) the meadow to reach the corner of the woods on the far side (sketchmap 3.4) then walk alongside the fence uphill to reach a gate. Through the gate bear right (WSW) and aim at the summit of Yr Eifl, the mountain with the mine workings on its eastern flank. This brings you to a copse some 200 yards away. A stile leads into the trees, and an obvious path leads through to another stile.

Climb over the stile and bear left, now aiming for the col to the left of the summit of Yr Eifl. Pass by a corner of a fence and then follow the fence uphill to a gate leading onto a lane (OS Ref: 371459).

This $^{1}/_{2}$ mile section between the two roads is waymarked and will present no problems, other than those in the woods at the bottom, if that route is chosen. The route arrives at the top road by a house and outbuildings. This is in fact a small pottery and you can view, and buy the pottery on show in the barn.

The way lies right (NW) along the lane for 300 yards until it reaches a high point and turns abruptly right and starts to drop down to Trefor. At this point (OS Ref: 368463) an unmade track goes off to the left (SW) and climbs up the hillside towards the col above.

The climb is quite steep, gaining nearly 800ft in $^{3}/_{4}$ mile. The landscape becomes increasingly wild and the vegetation is dominated by heather. The trail is however perfectly clear. Starting up the obvious lane a kissing gate is soon reached. Keep on up the track passing a ruined house to a further gate giving access to the open moor. The track becomes narrower but the way moves towards the telegraph poles and then trends right to reach the col. Those who have sprinted up without pause should now turn round and survey the view for it is very fine, taking the eye back along the northern coast to the entrance to the Menai Straits. Mere mortals who have paused for breath during the ascent will no doubt have noticed the increasingly good views as they progressed.

At the top of the col the obvious but fairly narrow track joins a wide cart track, which leads over the top continuing south-west (OS Ref: 362454). Even in poor conditions the route is now plain. It is also possible to take a diversion to the summit of Yr Eifl for a good track leads from the top of the col, south up the heather clad hillside to the summit. Follow the cart track as it gently descends across the western flanks of Yr Eifl. Soon, far below and to the right, can be seen the valley of Nant Gwrtheyrn.

Connections below Bwlch yr Eifl. The main route is designated as a bridleway

This is Vortigern's valley. Vortigern was a great prince of the 5th century who is supposed to have taken refuge in the valley to escape his enemies. Some accounts have it that his enemies were his own enraged subjects, so perhaps he was not such a great ruler. It seems that seeking refuge in the valley did not have the desired effect because Vortigern is supposed to have died here. Around 1750 a stone coffin was unearthed which contained an unusually large skeleton. The coffin was found in a tumulus called Bedd Gwrtheyrn and was thought to contain the remains of Vortigern.

This deep valley also has a much more sinister legend associated with it and although not part of the main coastal route is worth a visit. The legends of Nant Gwrtheyrn are related in circular walk (c) at the end of this chapter.

The track continues until, nearly 2 miles from the col at Bwlch yr Eifl, it reaches a tarmac lane running up from the village of Llithfaen (OS Ref: 353440). The main route continues straight ahead (SW) but to visit Nant Gwrtheyrn turn right along the road to drop into the valley. Alternatively, to reach the village of Llithfaen turn left along the road and down the hill. (See photograph.)

The main route goes straight across the tarmac passing over a somewhat boggy section to reach a gate in a wall signed by a bridleway symbol. Pass through the gate and walk alongside the fence bearing slightly left to a further gate at a fence junction. Through the gate a short green lane appears and in a few yards a sharp left and right turn leads to a gate in a wall. The gate leads out into open hillside with only a faint track heading west-south-west.

In 400 yards a gate in a fence is seen to the left (S) just by a low bank. The gate is waymarked. Pass through the gate and drop to the right to walk alongside a drystone wall. A gate soon appears in the wall to the right and having gone through it keep walking alongside the wall until a metal stile is seen. The wall which the stile crosses is very broken and gaps make the stile redundant. Nevertheless the stile is a good pointer because you must now turn right down the hill.

The OS map shows the right of way staying close by the wall but a reasonable track has developed which trends away from the wall to the left and drops to a stile at a farm lane. Eagle-eyed mapreaders will note that the 1:25,000 map does in fact show a footpath (not designated as a right of way) on the line of the track. Purists who wish to stay on the actual right of way reach the farm lane 80 yards north of the stile but are faced with a fence. The easiest choice seems to be to bow to the inevitable and use the track and the stile.

At the farm lane turn right (N) and pass over a cattle grid when a waymarked stile is seen on the left near a signpost to Pystyll. Climb over the stile and stay by the fence to reach another farm lane by a gate and some conifers. Keep right towards the farm, named as Ciliau-uchaf (OS Ref: 341432). As the first cottage comes up on the left take the gate also on the left to pass behind the cottage. Cross what appears to be the lawn for the cottage trending left to reach another gate leading to a sunken lane.

Walk between the banks of the lane for 100 yards to emerge onto the open hillside. In the distance a raised bank can be seen. Keep walking in a straight line taking the direction from the line of the sunken lane. As you get nearer to the raised bank a stile can be seen. Cross over the stile onto the open moor. At this point the moor is slightly convex, so no further landmarks are visible but walk up the hillside tending slightly left (WSW)

Pistyll

The descent to Pistyll Church

until on cresting the rise a fence can be seen with a stile. (The only clue to the correct route before the crest is reached is a line of telegraph poles, the way lying under the wires.)

Clamber over the stile then walk down the fence on the left, ignoring gateways until the fence bears right to reach a stile by a gateway. Over the stile keep in the same direction with a stone bank to the left and still ignoring gates soon reach another stile by the houses at Cefnydd (OS Ref: 333424).

Continue in the same direction, keeping above the buildings, and walk alongside a fence to yet another stile, which is waymarked. The way continues alongside the fence which soon curves round to the right to reach a gate by a short stretch of wall. Pass through the gate to emerge onto the top of a narrowing ridge covered in bracken. This is Cefnydd Hill, the significance of which is mentioned below. The track is plain and soon curves round to the left to drop off the ridge and zigzag down to a stile at the side of a lane (OS Ref: 329423). The lane and the stile can be seen from *the top of the ridge making the final descent straightforward (see photograph). On reaching the lane turn right. In 100 yards the lane curves to the left and Pistyll church can be seen ahead. The church is worth a visit as it has historical connections with the Bardsey Pilgrims.*

Pistyll Church

The church is dedicated to St. Beuno of whom mention has already been made in connection with the church at Clynnog, and the legend of St. Winifred. This site became a hospice church and was another important stopping point for those en route to Bardsey. In the Dark and Middle Ages there was, in addition to the church, a monastery, an inn and a hospice which was situated on Cefnydd Hill which followers of the main route have just walked over. There is precious little to be seen of these places now. The hospice covered an area of some 20 acres with a number of huts for those who wished

The little church at Pistyll marks the site of a hospital and earlier church which provided spiritual and physical comforts to the pilgrims.

to recuperate. A smaller section was dedicated to those suffering from leprosy.

The original church was probably made from wood, plaster and thatch with a circular boundary fence. The early Celtic monks were succeeded by white friars who were probably Cistercian. The date of the original settlement is not known but at some stage the early wood building was replaced by a more substantial stone construction. The stone church would have been square in shape and included a lepers window. This was a window set at such an angle that lepers could remain outside, yet watch the proceedings and receive sacrament through the window without the risk of infecting the rest of the congregation. They are found in several older churches in Wales.

The original door was in the present day south wall of the church and the original step can be seen in the wall. The oldest artefact is the font which is of Celtic origin. The symbols on the font are meant to depict everlasting life. The churchyard itself is now oval in shape but there are still the signs of plants which would at one time have been used for medical purposes. Thus Hop vines and Danesberry can still be found; the latter was reputed to assist the soul's journey in the hereafter.

The church was restored in 1949 under the direction of the Rev. Thomas Michaelionas. At this time a mural was discovered dating from the 14th century, which may depict St. Christopher. Also found was the inscription "Alleluia" and the Roman numerals "DDL" which would equate to the year 1050 AD. Those who wish to learn more of the history of the church will find further details in the church itself.

One further point of interest to modern man is the grave of Rupert Davies which can be found at the high side of the churchyard to the east of the building. Rupert Davies became famous on television in the 1960s for his portrayal of the French detective, Maigret.

To continue in the footsteps of the early pilgrims leave the church and walk south-west down the road, over a stream to reach the drive to a hotel (see sketchmap 3.5). There is a sign saying "Hotel & Y-Dorlan only". The hotel has been disused for some time but there are signs of restoration work being undertaken. Walk along the drive to the hotel (OS Ref: 327423)

where a kissing gate indicates
the way ahead. Pass through
and keep close to the wall,
ignoring a stile on the right,
to reach a wall junction with
a further stile which leads
over on to a wide track.

The track leads to a small
residence to the right,
however the way does not take
the wide track but crosses
straight over it to reach a gap
in a low wall directly ahead,
on the seaward side of a small
knoll. The gap is not easy to
discern but having gained a
little height a stile comes into
view to show the way (see
photograph p50). Contour
around the hillside above a

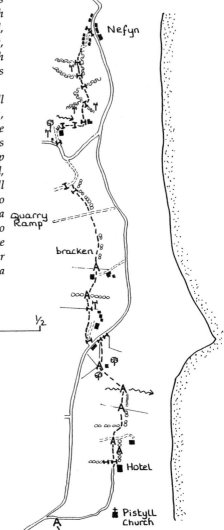

Pistyll to Nefyn
Sketchmap 3.5

Half a mile south-west of Pistyll church an inviting track appears to lead down to the sea. The correct route ignores it; as shown on the photograph

low bank then bear right to a stile in a gully. Climb out of the gully and then bear left towards some trees and a ruined cottage. Curving round the landward side of the ruin leads you to a rather overgrown stile. From the stile a fence lies south-west and should be followed until you are funnelled into a gate which leads out on to the main road by a bus stop (OS Ref: 322418). (NB. The OS map shows the right of way on the landward side of the fence, but this gives no access to the road, walkers should keep to the seaward side of the fence.)

The town of Nefyn is now only about a mile away along the road and it is tempting to turn right and stroll down into the town. However the road can be avoided by connecting a series of footpaths just to the south, but there have been changes in recent years to the rights of way so care must be taken. In addition parts of the route, in best guidebook parlance "will benefit from being walked more frequently" - this is code for "vastly overgrown"! How difficult the

Connection between Pistyll and Nefyn. The route turns off the drive to Ty Mawr onto a short green lane.

section will be depends on the time of year, because the problems are caused by bracken. Thus if it is April or early May the problems will not be great; if it is September be prepared for a fight!

To reach Nefyn by footpath turn left (E) at the main road, that is away from Nefyn, but in 50 yards cross over the road and turn into a gravel drive at Ty Mawr. Pass through the gate and start along the drive but after a few yards bear left onto a green ramp going into the trees (see photograph). The access to the ramp is a little overgrown, but once on it a track appears. Other tracks lead off left up the hill but ignore these and stay low in the woods.

Through the trees to the right can be seen a farmhouse and barns and the way continues in the trees above the farm buildings. Soon the trees end and the vegetation changes to gorse. The correct line is still low, aiming for a telegraph pole situated above an animal pen made of breeze blocks. A gate will be found just by the pole. Pass through the gate and follow the line given by the telephone wires to reach a stone stile and a small swing gate. This is the point where the right of way changes have been made by a diversion order dated 7th April 1993.

From the swing gate follow an obvious trackline to emerge across the front of a house, with a stile directly ahead. The house is marked on the 1:25,000 map as Bodeilias (OS Ref: 318416). The overgrown section is next, so it is still possible to escape along the gravel lane which connects the house to the main road.

Cross in front of the house and over the stile. Depending on the time of year, now stroll gently alongside a low wall, or fight a path through chest high bracken to reach a high stone ramp which appears to bar further progress. The ramp was constructed to service the quarries on the hillside above but it crosses the line of the path, effectively blocking it.

The engineers who built the ramp did provide a way over for walkers by means of the biggest stone stile the author has ever seen, being about 15ft high. The steps are to the right as you approach the ramp but are not in a good state of repair. A safer, though awkward way is to climb up to the left, gaining a little height on the hillside before scrambling onto the ramp. This still leaves the problem of how to get down off the ramp, but fortunately the steps down on the other side (W) are in a much better state and appear sound. This would be a very difficult section with young children.

Having negotiated the ramp all problems are over. Follow an obvious track alongside a wall leading gently uphill until a gate is reached. Passing through the gate leads onto a wide cart track. Turn right. Stay on the cart track ignoring the lane leading off to the right until the track swings hard left. At this point go through a gate directly ahead which is the access to a cottage. Keep above the cottage then turn right down some steps to pass by the side of the cottage and through a white gate onto the open hillside. Drop to a kissing gate and then bear right down the side of a stream until a further kissing gate appears on the left by the house at Tyn-y-Cae (OS Ref: 313410).

Go through the gate and pass under telephone wires to reach a hedge. Turn right, and walk alongside the hedge to a gate. Pass through and then bear left, passing under the telephone wires again to a further gate in a hedge. A few yards further on is another gate and the way continues alongside the line of telegraph poles. A kissing gate is soon reached and after keeping by the hedgeline for a few yards an opening appears on the right which leads onto a footpath between houses to emerge on the main road in Nefyn (OS Ref: 309408).

Nefyn Harbour
The trade in stone from the inland quarries died many years ago, and the
harbours of the northern Lleyn towns are now used only for a few fishing boats
and pleasure craft

CYCLISTS

Cyclists can follow this section by using a mixture of lanes and bridleways. It is not possible to keep to the exact line followed by the walkers, but there are some exhilarating sections, and the climb and descent over the Rivals will test many riders.

From Penygroes follow the main route on the cycleway in common with the walkers. Where the route leaves the cycleway there is something of a dilemma, as the short connection is strictly a footpath. It is necessary either to carry your bike for a few yards across the field to the lane, or to abandon the cycleway 100 yards before the walkers and climb up to the lane as it crosses the railway.

The route then continues as described for the walkers to the village of Tai'n-lôn. The whole track over the shoulder of the hill is classed as a RUPP or Road Used as a Public Path. Thus cyclists are entitled to use this way, though in places there are precious few signs of a "road". Definitely a section for mountain bikes!

Cyclists must go a slightly longer way than the walkers to leave Tai'n-lôn. Cycle along the lane past the footpath sign and the low cottage for about 200 yards to a point where the road sweeps gently right and there is a turn-off to the left down to the river, past a small private garage. Purists can cycle through the ford if they wish, others may prefer the little footbridge, to reach a 'Y' junction on the now unsurfaced track. The left-hand track leads up to an old building.

To continue the route take the right fork at the ford to a gate leading onto the open hillside. There is a private house on the right but the way lies left (SW) through the gate and up the steep hill. There is a depression close to the fence which marks the way. This route is classed as another RUPP but if you can manage to pedal all the way up to the gate at the top of the depression then you have considerable leg muscles.

At the top the gate leads into a small walled enclosure. If you have pedalled all the way you are allowed to collapse here! The enclosure has four gates - exit from the one opposite to the gate by which you entered to gain a green lane. Pass through two gates and by the farm of Bryn Hafod and then by the farm lane to reach the road at Pont Rhyd-y-beirion (OS Ref: 436497) just a few yards west of where the walkers arrived.

Turn left along the lane, past the drive to the farm at Maesog, to a lane junction where a right turn (S) is made, signed "Pensarn 4". Cycle up the hill to reach a left-hand dogleg in the road and so arrive 30 yards further on at a road junction. Turn right and pedal uphill to a 'T' junction (OS Ref: 437483) just north of an obvious radio mast.

Cyclists and walkers now part company for some miles. The next 3 miles or so are a delight for the walker passing over the shoulder of Bwlch Mawr, but unhappily for the cyclist the right of way is designated as only a footpath, and in any case is quite steep in the initial stages. Cyclists therefore must turn right (NNW) at the 'T' junction and descend to the village of Clynnog.

Unhappily there are no suitable off-road connections between Clynnog and Trefor and cyclists must therefore follow the A499 road for about 3 miles before they can turn off into the village of

Trefor.

From the main road a right turn (OS Ref: 385467) leads into the surprisingly large village of Trefor. Follow the road past the big church (sketchmap 3.4) until a general stores and newsagent (Siop Glandwr) appears on the left opposite some public toilets. Take the next right and immediately the first left. From the general store the signs to the Plas yr Eifl hotel show the right way.

Cycle up the hill to a 'Y' junction, the right-hand branch signed to Plas yr Eifl Hotel and the left-hand branch signed to Cwm Pottery. Take the left-hand branch. To ensure identification there is a road called Stryd Sychnant on the right and a cottage called Cae Cropa on the left just before the 'Y' junction.

Climb steeply uphill until the lane suddenly turns to the left and levels out. An unmade track lies directly in front, and is designated such that bicycles can be legitimately used. Walkers and cyclists are now together again facing the stiff pull to the col at Bwlch yr Eifl (OS Ref: 362454). The track is steep and in the form of a narrow lane until the second gate is reached. The track then gives onto the open moor but the line is shown by the row of telegraph poles. The track becomes quite narrow near the top, but it is always distinct. Soon a good unmade lane is reached and the way lies to the left.

Cyclists continue on the main route now, with a fast descent on the west side of the col to arrive at the lane leading up from Llithfaen (OS Ref: 354440). The OS map and the signposts confirm that the continuation across the lane is a bridleway, but be warned that it is boggy and far less easy to follow than the track down from the col. (Those who have had enough excitement for the time being can turn left down the lane to the village of Llithfaen to meet the main road where a right turn is made.)

Whichever way riders choose they arrive on the main road just west of the farm at Tan-y-bwlch (OS Ref: 344429). Drop down the hill for just over ¹/₂ mile, where the road swings suddenly to the right around a spur. The road continues west, dropping less steeply until a narrow lane is seen off to the right (NW).

This lane leads down to Pistyll church, the history of which is described in the main walking section above. After viewing the church it is necessary to return to the main road.

Continue for ¹/₂ mile into the village of Pistyll when a minor road goes off on the left (OS Ref: 325418). The junction is marked by a chapel and Penisarlon Farm on the right. Turn left up the lane and climb past the school. The lane is quite steep, but in $^1/_2$ mile the gradient eases and drops very gently downhill. Just by the bungalow called Rhosydd a little lane goes off to the right (OS Ref: 331412). Some maps show this as an unmade 'white' road but in fact it is surfaced throughout its length. Enthusiasts will be able to go off-road by cycling along the grass strip in the middle of the lane!

This excellent high level lane contours the south side of Carreglefain and provides superb views across the whole countryside. The lane starts to drop and comes to a 'T' junction by a phone box. Turn right and descend into Nefyn. Those wishing to avoid the climb around Carreglefain can stay on the main road at Pistyll and reach Nefyn easily, but with lesser views.

OTHER WALKS IN THIS AREA

a) The hill forts of Yr Eifl

Start:	Road junction 1 mile east of Llithfaen
Car park:	Possibilities at side of road
OS Ref:	367434
Distance:	3 miles (5 with extension)
Height:	800ft (1300 with extension)
Grade:	A

The triple peaks of the Rivals have been in view for much of the walk along the North Coast. It would be a pity then not to explore them, especially as one summit has one of the best examples of a hill fort to be seen anywhere in the country. This hill fort not only displays the ramparts, which are common on so many hill forts, but also the original walls and the circular huts which are plain to see. Once started on the walk across these mountains it is easy to see why they have lain so undisturbed over the centuries, for this is a genuinely wild area. In total area these mountains are tiny compared to the expanse of their more famous Snowdonian brothers, but the terrain is as wild as anywhere in the national park. They are reminiscent of the Rhinogs.

This gives the clue not to set out over this area without proper

The hill fort of Yr Eifl.
The start of the walk from the Nefyn to Llanaelhaearn road.

mountain equipment. The walks may be short but the weather can
change rapidly with squalls rushing in from the Irish Sea. Underfoot
the country is difficult with much heather moor, and the tracks,
though mostly obvious, are narrow.

To visit the hill fort start 200 yards west of the highest point on
the B4417 road which drops down to Nefyn (OS Ref: 367434). Here
a gate and a footpath sign show the way (see photograph). Climb
steeply up the grassy hillside on a faint track aiming for a large and
obvious crag on the hillside above. Cross the fence via a stile and
continue to the base of the crag. Here the track splits. Turn right and
walk under the crag. The track is indistinct but soon improves.

Contour the hill and bear left until a drystone wall blocks the
way. Follow the wall uphill to a stile by a portacabin! (What such a
structure is doing in this wild setting is anybody's guess and one can
only speculate on how it was brought here.) Climb over the stile and
drop down the hill for a few yards to turn left onto a track. This
crosses a flat, wet area but soon joins a more substantial track. Keep
left and follow the track steeply to the summit. The hill fort and its

associated dwellings are plain to see and there is a plaque giving brief details.

It is worth walking over to the eastern side of the summit. The view from this point shows how well the fort was defended on this side, the hillside being particularly steep. The village of Trefor can be seen nestling far below and there are excellent views along the whole coastline back to Caernarfon.

The fort however did not occupy the highest summit of the area and the main summit of Yr Eifl can be seen to the north-west. If you have good footwear it is worth the effort to cross the col and ascend the spur which leads to the top. Be warned that there are few tracks and it is really a matter of picking your own route across the wild moor.

For the less hardy the ascent should be reversed until the stile by the portacabin is reached. To add some variety and provide good views over Nefyn do not retrace the steps down the wall but carry straight on across the moor on a good track. This soon starts to lose height and a stile comes into view. Do not cross the stile (but note the next paragraph) but some 40 yards before it pick up a track peeling off to the left and follow this as it curves around the mountainside. It drops to a fence and leads back to the stile at the start of the walk. Climb over the stile and drop down the grass to reach the road.

The stile noted above gives access to a track which drops into the village of Llithfaen. For those without their own transport this allows the walk to be done from the village, which is on a bus route. In this case the ascent to and descent from the hill fort are made on the same tracks and this adds nearly 2 miles to the round trip.

b) Clynnog-fawr Circular

Start:	Main A499 road 300yds NE of Pont y Felin
Car park:	An old and unused section of road
OS Ref:	406488
Distance:	5 miles
Height:	2170ft
Grade:	A

An excellent outing with something for everyone. There can be few places left in Wales where there is a waterfall over 100ft high that is not surrounded by the trappings of tourism, but there is one on this walk. Add to that delightful mixed woodland, wild flowers, deserted open hillsides and glorious views and it makes you wonder why this area is so overlooked.

The route starts along the farm track at the eastern end of the lay-by that has been created by the old road. Walk along the track passing the farm at Cwmgwared (OS Ref: 408486) and aiming into the valley ahead. The track soon enters trees by a cottage and then climbs steadily above a delightful river. The track is plain as it wends its way through the woodland, but soon steepens and a large waterfall is seen on the right. The foliage in summer masks much of the falls which are best seen after rain in the early spring.

The track becomes less distinct but the way lies parallel to the river until the mountain wall is reached at the top of the woods. The stone stile which once gave access to the hillside above has collapsed but the wall can be easily stepped over at the point it drops to meet the river.

Cross over on to the open hillside keeping the stream on the right for 100 yards or so until striking east up the grass to attain the summit of Bwlch Mawr (OS Ref: 427478). This is a good viewpoint and especially to the south-west demonstrates just how hilly the Lleyn peninsula is, contrary to popular opinion.

Drop off the summit to the south and thus pick up the track which crosses the south flank of the hill. This is clearly marked on the OS map, and is part of the main route around the Lleyn. Turn west on the track but only to the point where it forms a green lane between two drystone walls. (OS Ref: 416466). Here turn north and follow the line of the wall into the head of the valley. The wall soon turns to the left (WSW) and the route turns with it.

Ahead now is the broad saddle between the summits of Gyrn Ddu and Gyrn Goch. Walk across the grass to the low point of the saddle. A drystone wall is found just over the crest and a right turn (NNE) should be made to walk alongside the wall to the summit of Gyrn Goch, another fine viewpoint. Drop off the summit towards the sea (NNW), crossing over the drystone wall as it leaves the summit (sketchmap 3.6 p60 and photograph p61). Walk very steeply

The descent from Gyrn Goch
Sketchmap 3.6

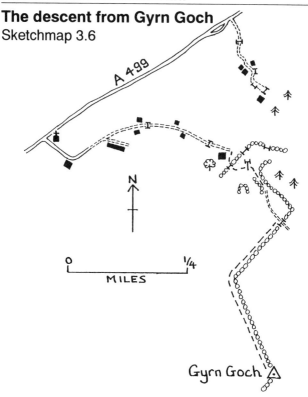

down the wall on a faint track. The wall turns to the right (NE) after 400 yards and the route turns with it. Keep hard by the wall until a gate appears on the right. On the left at this point is an obvious track so turn left down it. The track stays parallel to the tree plantation until it winds into a short stretch of green lane.

The green lane opens out into a small meadow with a number of gorse bushes. Bear left across the meadow, passing a telegraph pole, to reach the higher of two gates in a wall. Pass through the gate and walk below a house on an obvious track (OS Ref: 403484). Pass through a gate onto a green lane and a further gate when the track becomes a road. Pass by the cottages and take the lane as it curves

The descent from Gyrn Goch

to the right at the house called Tyn y Ffynnon to drop down to the main road. Turn right and walk back to the start of the walk.

c) Nant Gwrtheyrn

Start:	Llithfaen
Car park:	$1/2$ mile north of village
OS Ref:	356432
Distance:	3 miles (less from car park)
Height:	1100ft (900 from car park)
Grade:	B (due to steepness of climb)

The legend of Nant Gwrtheyrn is a terrible and morbid one. The valley itself is a narrow defile cutting down to the sea. Many years ago a small village prospered at the bottom of the valley. However its inhabitants were heathen, and attracted three monks from St. Beuno's church at Clynnog, who were set on converting the residents.

The monks were not well received and the villagers drove them out of the village. As a last act of defiance the monks threw a triple curse on the village.

The first curse said that no one dying in the village would ever lie in consecrated ground; the second curse said that no man and woman from the village could ever marry each other; and the third that the village would become desolate.

The first curse appeared fulfilled when for many years people from the village disappeared on death. They died by falling over the cliffs or by drowning and thus were never buried.

So careful were the inhabitants about the second curse that they sought partners from outside the village. Nevertheless in due course two lovers from the village decided to get married. A local tradition was that the bride should pretend to be coy and hide herself on the wedding morning. The groom's friends would then seek her out to take her to the church. The bride duly obliged but the groomsmen could not find her. As with all good stories the groom died of a broken heart. Many years later a violent thunderstorm hit the village and a bolt of lightning split an old oak tree revealing a skeleton dressed in bridal robes - the girl had hidden in a cleft of the tree and become entrapped.

The third curse seemed most unlikely to be fulfilled and in the 19th century the village prospered and expanded. Soon however the quarrying declined and the village fell on hard times. By 1960 the village was deserted, a ruin, and the third curse had come to pass.

After such stories you may not wish to visit the place at all but perhaps the curse is now broken for the village has in the last ten years seen a revival and is the site of a training centre for the furtherance of the Welsh language. Perhaps St. Beuno would have approved of the new use of the village, but then again perhaps those who work there now should, if such a situation arises, get married in Nefyn!

The walk starts from the village of Llithfaen, although if you are travelling by car a mile or so can be saved by driving up to the shoulder of Yr Eifl where there is adequate parking. This is the point where the main Pilgrims Route crosses the lane.

From the parking place walk down the road which is very steep.

It takes some 20 minutes to descend to the village. There is also the option of following the black waymarks which provide a route through the trees. Apart from the occasional mining relic the valley is very pleasant whichever route is chosen, and the village soon comes into view.

The last inhabitants left the village in 1959, and the buildings rapidly became derelict. In 1978 the village was developed as a Welsh language centre, and all the buildings were renovated. In addition to the accommodation for those attending courses there is a small museum, a cafe and a chapel.

To extend the walk it is possible to go right down to the beach. The trouble needed to get to this beach at least means that it is very quiet. The western end of the beach has relics of the Porth-y-Nant quarry and unusually the remains of a second world war landing craft. It is possible to extend the walk to include the whole of the Nant Gwrtheyrn Trail. (Booklets describing this longer circular walk are available in the little museum.) The only problem with the visit to the village is that, unlike most walks, you have to finish with a stiff climb back to the starting point.

CHAPTER 4
Nefyn to Aberdaron

Chapter 3 leaves you at the entrance to the town of Nefyn. It appears to be just a normal seaside town, but in fact has a long history. In 1224 Edward I finally subjugated the Welsh princes by his victory over Llywelyn the Last. In celebration of his victory he held a tournament at Nefyn. In 1355 Nefyn became one of only ten Royal Boroughs in Wales. Unfortunately precious little of this era survives.

The main old church is St. Mary's, which can be seen to the left as you enter the town. It has a slim tower which is surmounted by a very large and disproportionate ship, a sign of the town's relationship with fishing. The ship does duty as a weathercock. Inside the church is a tablet which bears the inscription "Here lieth the body of Ellen Wynne .. wife of John Parry of Nevin. She died in 1679 aged about 100". This highlights the old, and long disused, Welsh custom of the wife retaining her maiden name after marriage.

The main route does not enter the centre of Nefyn, and so those who wish to seek out overnight accommodation, cafes, pubs and other delights of the flesh will need to stay on the main road and stroll the couple of hundred yards into the main part of the town.

From the point where the footpath arrives at the main road turn left (W) along the road and stay on it, ignoring all side roads until the main road itself swings to the left (sketchmap 4.1). At this point a minor lane comes in from the right and leads past the obvious landmark of the fire station. Stay on the main road around the left-hand bend but in just a few yards a footpath sign points off right between shops. The path runs alongside the shop called Studio Crafts.

On clearing the buildings bear left and after 20 yards turn right, keeping the steel tower on the right, to reach a 'T' junction. Turn left. (This point can also be reached by another right of way which passes behind the fire station.)

Follow the obvious track, ignoring a footpath to the left and then one to the right (which gives access only to the beach) to emerge on a residential road (OS Ref: 304407). Turn to the right (SW) and reach a 'T' junction.

View north east across Traeth Penllech
Porth Colmon

Aberdaron village
Y Gegin Fawr - pilgrim's stop at Aberdaron

Y Gegin Fawr
The Big Kitchen

BUILT 1300 A.D. WHERE THE SAINTS
COULD CLAIM A MEAL BEFORE
CROSSING THE SOUND TO
BARDSEY ISLAND.

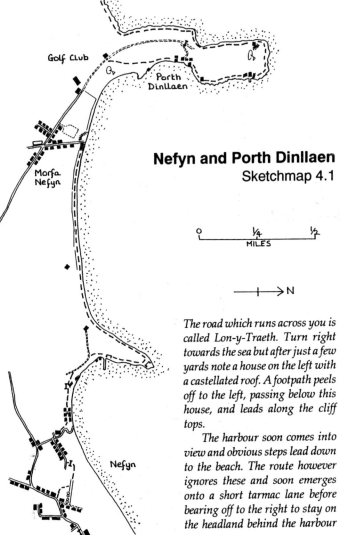

Nefyn and Porth Dinllaen
Sketchmap 4.1

The road which runs across you is called Lon-y-Traeth. Turn right towards the sea but after just a few yards note a house on the left with a castellated roof. A footpath peels off to the left, passing below this house, and leads along the cliff tops.

The harbour soon comes into view and obvious steps lead down to the beach. The route however ignores these and soon emerges onto a short tarmac lane before bearing off to the right to stay on the headland behind the harbour

Yr Eifl from Morfa Nefyn

wall. *Purists will wish to walk the track which takes them right round the headland, and they will be rewarded by fine views from the tip of the headland. Those pressed for time can save a few minutes by cutting across the neck of the headland. Either way the paths are plain.*

The next mile is a delight, following the cliff top with good views over to Porth Dinllaen and the headland jutting out from the little hamlet. Steps eventually lead down to a road where there are toilets. Directly opposite the steps is a footpath sign showing the way continuing on the cliff top, but this is not shown as a right of way on the OS map. To stay legal, at least as far as the OS are concerned, turn left and walk up the road (S) to the crossroads at the Linksway Hotel (OS Ref: 283406). Turn right. See sketchmap 4.1.

Once again there are opportunities at this point to divert into civilisation in the shape of Morfa Nefyn, a smaller relative of Nefyn but with similar facilities. This is the last place of any size before Aberdaron. To reach the main part of the town turn left at the Linksway Hotel, or, to continue the route, turn right.

Follow the lane towards the golf club. There is a sign which states this is a private road, but it is a right of way on foot. Walk past the coastguard buildings and the clubhouse and continue in the same direction (NW) along an obvious track until a small hut appears on the left. At this point bear right up the grassy bank and to the left of a green to reach the crest of the small ridge where bushes and bramble take over from the well kept fairways of the golf course, and the sea comes into view. Drop down on the seaward side following a narrow but clear path to reach the hamlet of Porth Dinllaen.

Most visitors will agree that Porth Dinllaen is very different from Holyhead, but there is a connection between this tiny hamlet and the large bustling town on Anglesey. In the early 1800s Porth Dinllaen was under consideration as the site for the main port to link with Ireland. The attraction was the obvious shelter given by the headland, and the deepwater harbour possibilities.

In fact work started on the approaches, and a glance at a map of the Lleyn peninsula shows the straight road which was constructed from Pwllheli to Morfa Nefyn, which is now the main A487. This stretch of road was meant to be the final stage of a super highway running all the way from London. However despite the investment in this road no work was ever done on the harbour.

Later in the 18th century interest in Porth Dinllaen was revived when the Great Western railway company sketched out plans to lay a wide gauge line from Worcester, and open up the hamlet as the port it had been intended to be. In the event the Chester to Holyhead route was favoured, mainly because the problem of getting over the Menai Straits and the Conwy river had by then been solved by Telford's success with his two chain bridges.

Nevertheless, even as late as 1878 a tourist guide to the area still left the possibility open that Porth Dinllaen might be developed. Perhaps it is as well that all these schemes came to nothing. The magnificent coastal scenery hereabouts would hardly have been enhanced by all the paraphernalia of a modern port.

Pass through the hamlet where the cottages spring right out of the beach, and continue past the inn (OK, you can pause if you wish!) and between the cottages to reach a path on the eastern side of the headland. This delightful track stays low at the base of the cliffs to reach a lifeboat station (OS Ref: 278419).

At this point the path climbs up behind the station to the cliff tops and then continues round the headland with excellent views and rocky scenery. At the tip of the headland keep an eye open for the seals which bask on the rocks at the base of the cliffs. The path climbs again to rejoin the golf course as the right of way turns south to progress down the western side of the headland.

This side of the promontory is not as spectacular as the eastern side but the views along the coast have now been opened up and should whet the appetite for the route lies along the cliff tops which can be seen across the bay of Borth Wen. Follow the edge of the golf course, always overlooking the sea and curve round to the right (W).

At this point you may notice a small hut about 100 yards to the left. This is the same small hut which marked the turn off to Porth Dinllaen almost 2 miles ago! However it is NOT recommended to cut across the base of this headland as the walk around it is particularly scenic.

The next few miles are not only a delight to walk, but navigation is restricted to "keep the sea about 50 yards to the right". This part of the coast has been designated a Heritage Coast and the stiles, bridges and waymarks are all in a good state of repair. The ease of routefinding makes the need for sketchmaps superfluous and therefore maps in this section are restricted to showing access links at the southern end and opportunities for camping or overnight accommodation.

To start this section keep by the cliff edge on the side of the golf course until a little headland is reached. A golf tee sits atop the promontory. The way goes round the back of the tee and takes a path over a stile to drop into a bay, Aber Geirch (OS Ref: 266405), which would be a scenic delight except for the fact that a pipeline has been constructed through it. Cross the footbridge over the river and climb over the hillocks to leave the sounds of the golf course behind.

The route now parallels the shore, nearly always staying high on the cliff top, but making occasional forays down to sea level via steep little gullies which have been cut by streams as they drop down to reach the sea. The coastal views differ quite markedly from the sandy coloured cliffs of soft boulder clay to the dark, hard and ancient rocks which form the headlands. The bays in between the headlands are mostly deserted yet most have access to the lanes which run just inland and it is something of a surprise that the area has not been developed more. One hopes that its designation as a Heritage Coast will protect it from new developments and confirm its status as a quiet and lonely stretch of coast which is only readily accessible by those prepared to walk.

As an extra incentive the coast in this area is well endowed with wildlife, both flora and fauna. The wild flowers grow in profusion and many varieties can be found. Seabirds are common, of course, from the range of squeaking gulls to cormorants and oyster-catchers with their bright red bills. Rabbits are common as the soft boulder clay of parts of the cliff makes ideal burrowing conditions. Snakes can also be seen on warm days, basking on the rocks above the coves. They are quick to slither off into the undergrowth when they sense approaching footsteps.

There are no villages on the coast between Nefyn and Aberdaron which is a fair distance. This limits the possibilities for bed and breakfast to the occasional farm or cottage unless you are prepared to walk inland. Even then the only place of any size is Tudweiliog (OS Ref: 238368), where there is an inn and one or two establishments offering overnight accommodation. For those who choose to backpack the route the opportunities are more frequent, for there are small campsites at several points along the way.

From Aber Geirch with its unsightly pipeline stride out along the cliff tops with magnificent scenery all around. There is a fine natural arch after about 2 miles (OS Ref: 240390) and shortly after one of the gullies cutting across the cliffs is deeper than most and provides a good waterfall. Soon there are signs of civilisation at Rhos-y-llan (OS Ref: 237378) and you come across a small caravan park. This is Towyn Farm (OS Ref: 232375). For overnight camping cut inland through the caravans to see the farm at the side of a lane. This is a listed Camping and Caravanning Club site.

From the farm a footpath leads directly to the village of Tudweiliog in about 15 minutes. As previously noted the village has a small number of bed and breakfast establishments and an inn.

Continuing on the main route keep on the cliff top past the caravan site to reach the sandy bay of Porth Towyn, the biggest beach since Nefyn. Keep round the back of the bay to come across a small caravan site. The word 'site' is somewhat of an exaggeration for these are just a few caravans parked above a lonely bay. However they mark an access lane to the road, and by turning right (SW) along the road further camping can be found at Porthysgaden (OS Ref: 225371), about 10 minutes from the cliff top.

From the tiny caravan site a signpost shows the way to Port Ysgaden and the path swings north-west around a headland. On top of the headland is the ruin of some old but obviously large building. Drop off the headland round an inlet, Porth Ysgaden (OS Ref: 218374), to pass a couple of huts and a signpost to Porth Gwylan about ¹/₂ mile distant. Soon further signposts direct the way towards Traeth Penllech. At this sign to Traeth Penllech a cart track runs inland to a road and there is another Camping and Caravanning Club site at Tyddyn Sander (OS Ref: 221364) some 10 minutes' walk from the cliffs.

The main route continues along the cliff top and signs of civilisation disappear. The coastline is at first rocky but soon softens with more rolling grassy knolls becoming frequent until quite suddenly a headland is rounded and the large sandy expanse of Traeth Penllech comes into view. This is a magnificent bay, yet appears hardly used. The author has been on the beach on a hot sunny day in July and had the whole mile or so of sand to himself. The path stays on the crumbling cliff top some 60ft or so above the sands, until on reaching the far end of the bay you are forced down onto the beach itself.

At this point a signpost shows Porth Colmon in ¹/₂ mile, but it is worth a pause at this point, not only to view the fine sweep of the bay, but shortly after the sign a rocky gorge opens up in the cliffs.

A footpath leads into the gorge leading in 100 yards to a fine waterfall, shown in the photograph. The whole place is delightful, and one can easily see that such an enchanted grotto could lead to one of the tales about fairies for which rural Wales is famous.

Staying on the beach walk to the end of the bay where the path lies up a steep little spur back to the cliff tops. The top of this section is noteworthy for the wild orchids growing by the side of the path. The track soon reaches Porth Colmon (sketchmap 4.2), where for the first time in miles a road reaches the sea. Ten minutes along this road is Morfa (OS Ref: 198336) where there is a village store, a camping and caravan site (Moel y Berth) and a couple of houses providing B&B.

A little further inland on this same road is the church at Llangwnnadl (OS Ref: 209332). This is the last stopping place on the Pilgrims Route before reaching Aberdaron. The church itself is quite large and well kept. A short history inside confirms this as the site used by pilgrims from the 6th century onwards. Not far away is a good example of an early standing stone. These objects sometimes disappoint, being little more than a boulder. This one is a magnificent

Waterfalls at Traeth Penllech
As the ancient shoreline rises, the drop to the present day shoreline provides
some pleasant waterfalls. This is one of the best and is situated at
the southern end of Penllech beach.

71

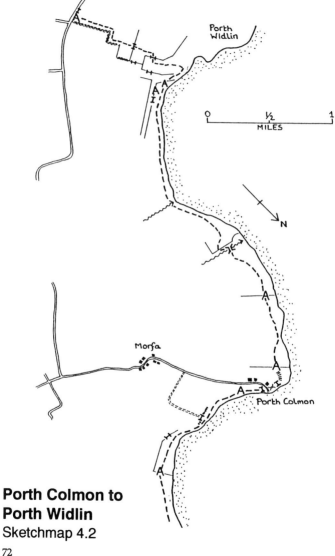

Porth
Widlin

0   ½   1
MILES

N

Morfa

Porth Colmon

**Porth Colmon to
Porth Widlin**
Sketchmap 4.2

Porth Colmon
For the first time in several miles a road reaches the coast at this point.
Walking inland along the road leads to the village of Morfa where there is
camping, a shop and one or two B&B establishments. The route continues
along the coast around the right-hand side of the stone cottage

example, a slender monolith some 10ft high. It can be seen in a field by the side of the Tudweiliog road at OS Ref: 208326.

The way ahead is past the right-hand side of a stone cottage at the end of the road, when steps assist in gaining height back onto the cliff top. Continue above a rocky shore for just over a mile. The footpath which has so unerringly kept by the sea now cuts inland. This is a great pity for there is some fine coastal scenery on the headlands to the west, but no right of way. Thus a short excursion inland must be made before picking up the coast path once again.

The turn-off point is easily missed, and reference should be made to sketchmap 4.2. Just after a boggy little section leading downhill there are two stiles virtually side by side. The left-hand leads to a track leading inland, but take the right-hand stile and bear right to descend a grassy rib (see photographs p74 & 75). A lonely little bay is now in sight, but a deep gully has to be crossed to reach it. The right of way leads away from the sea up the gully. See sketchmap 4.2.

Walk up the gully which is hemmed in at its top end by fences, but the path bears right (SW) to a gate. Pass through and turn immediately left

The standing stone at Llangwnnadl. This is a magnificent specimen standing some 10ft high

Approaching Porth Widlin Some care is needed in this area. The OS map shows two rights of way. The figure is climbing a new (1993) stile but this is NOT the best way. Keep straight on as shown until Porth Widlin itself comes into view

Porth Widlin
The small sandy cove of Porth Widlin marks the end of the right of way on this part of the north coast. A move inland must be made for the next 2 miles until paths lead back to the shore. The correct line is shown

(SE) following the fence for a few yards, but as the fence drops back stay in the same direction to reach another gate in a fence at the top of the field. Go through and still keeping on the same line soon reach a hedgerow. Walk alongside the hedgerow as it cuts right and then left to come to a gate and stile giving access to a narrow road (OS Ref: 186317). Turn right (SW).

It is somewhat galling to be walking on the road when excellent cliff tops are so near, but it is only for just over a mile and you are unlikely to encounter any traffic other than the odd tractor. The hedgerows provide some compensation and the wild roses are particularly fine.

Continue along the road ignoring turn-offs until a 'T' junction is reached at Ty-hen (OS Ref: 178310). Turn right (W). After a few yards the road splits and the way is by the left-hand fork.

The right-hand fork should not be dismissed, however, as it

leads in ¹/₂ mile to the site of the ancient church of St. Menin. There is no building to see, just a fenced off mound in the middle of a field. It is not clear whether this was yet another holy site on the Pilgrims Route to Bardsey mainly because of the difficulty of finding information about St. Menin. It is possible that this is a corruption of the saint known as Merin. Given that St. Merin was also known as Meirin, Merini and Myrini it appears possible that this ancient site has the same connection.

This possibility seems to be confirmed by the fact that St. Merin is the patron saint of the parish of Bodferin. The house of Plas Bodferin is just over ¹/₂ mile east of the site, and it is known that the old parish of Bodferin was very small, running for just a mile along the coast. In 1901 it had only 49 parishioners. Boundaries were later redrawn to provide for a bigger and more viable unit.

The site is now on private land but can be seen easily from the road. This branch of the road also gives access to Porth Iago, a superb rocky cove which is well worth a visit and gives an idea of what is being missed by having to walk the lanes inland.

The main route continues along the left-hand fork and in ¹/₂ mile a bridleway is seen on the right leading down to Porth Oer, more commonly known as the Whistling Sands. The bridleway is marked by two gates suspended on large cylindrical gateposts. Drop onto the beach and walk south to the far end of the bay.

The name Whistling Sands is given because of the reputed noise made by the sand when it is walked over. Apparently the grains of sand are of such a shape that when pressed together by the pressure of the foot they emit a squeaking or whistling sound. The author has to admit that despite walking along the whole length of the beach on several occasions he has never heard the sound.

At the south-west end of the bay walk past the little cafe and clamber onto the rocks when an obvious path appears. Here will be found waymarks in the shape of a Celtic cross and such markers now appear at regular intervals all the way to the headland opposite Bardsey Island. Whether the pilgrims followed this narrow track so close to the sea or trod easier lanes inland is a moot point, but the waymarked track has some fine scenery.

It will be noted that the OS map shows no rights of way over this particular section of coast, but the land is owned by the National Trust and you are free to follow the path.

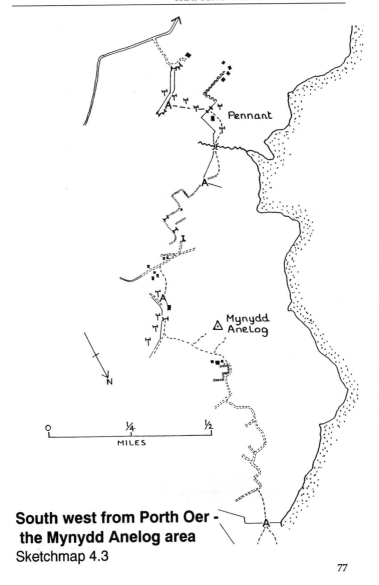

South west from Porth Oer -
the Mynydd Anelog area

Sketchmap 4.3

The track crosses a stile with a signpost to Anelog and then contours the cliffside passing the island of Dinas Bach (OS Ref: 157294), which is only a true island at high water, to reach a bridge over a narrow cleft. Cross the bridge and the stile ahead. The track now contours the hillside but it is narrow and cuts across a steep slope. Those of a nervous disposition or with youngsters should abandon the path and gain height to the left onto the crest where, for a while, a fence marks the way.

The narrow path eventually peters out and those hardy souls who have followed this route should also now strike up the hill to the crest and by following the line of the coast reach a stile where the track improves again. Those who have avoided the narrow track also reach this stile. The way leads uphill over the stile (sketchmap 4.3) and the track improves as it goes. It crests the headland with good views in all directions and then drops to a very obvious cart track. Turn right (SW) along the cart track.

There are a number of cart tracks on this hillside, which make navigation easy as long as the correct turns are made. At the first 'Y' junction bear right and again, in a few yards, keep right at the next junction. Soon a track comes in from the left but keep straight on to a 'T' junction and again turn right. The track now leads alongside a walled garden area with a white cottage behind. Keep on the track until it swings left towards the cottage then cut off right up the hill on a narrower path. This soon crests a rise and improves.

There are some lesser tracks off to the right. The main route ignores these, but for those with energy they can be followed to the summit of Mynydd Anelog, the hill on the right. The exertion of the ascent is well worth the effort. The view from the top of Mynydd Anelog ranges from Aberdaron round to Bardsey itself.

The main track gently loses height and drops to a fence where there is a signpost pointing the way to Braich y pwll. Keep in the same direction alongside the fence to pass through a gate as you approach a building and some tin sheds. The cart track starts to swing to the left. Take care, for the way drops off this track on the right to cross over a stile.

Cross over the trackless pasture in much the same direction, keeping some barns on your left, to reach another cart track. Turn right. Very soon a crossroads is reached. Go straight across. The next few hundred yards are not obvious, but the Celtic cross waymarks help in finding the correct line, which is also indicated on sketchmap 4.3. Go along the track, ignore a gate on the right but pass through a gate as the line of the path bends slightly left. Keep by the left-hand field edge (a bank marks the line) to a gate by a Celtic marker.

Do not pass through the gate but turn right alongside the bank and fence. The bank soon cuts back to the left. Keep on the same line as the last 50 yards and aim for a solitary white cottage at the base of the hill opposite. A bank is soon rejoined and keeping by it leads to a stile. Go over and immediately turn right down some steps. An overgrown and quite steep track then leads down to the stream in the little valley.

Cross the stream by the bridge and climb up the hill to a gate marked "Pennant". Note that there is a Celtic marker before the stile which indicates a faint track to the right, this should be ignored as it leads only to a viewpoint above the cliffline. Through the gate aim for the telegraph pole in front. The track curves right as it reaches the pole and then left in an arc to reach the next telegraph pole behind a cottage. A gate appears. Go through the gate into a field and keep on the line of the telegraph poles to reach a gate and stile on the far side of the field. (The position of the stile is just left of the line of the poles.)

The stile gives access to a farm track. Turn right to reach a gate by some barns. Pass through onto the farm access lane and turn left. The lane soon leads to a public road where a right turn is made. There is a campsite on the left (Camping and Caravanning Club). Stay on the road until a cattle grid is crossed where a wide track bears off left and drops down a small valley.

You are now very close to the end of the peninsula, and soon the North Coast will be abandoned to start the walk east along the South Coast of the Lleyn. This is a very popular spot, the "Land's End" of North Wales. There are car parks, marker boards with points of interest laid out, and picnic spots. The track down the small valley is therefore well trod and plain to see.

Walk down the track, crossing the little stream to reach the bare rock. Steps have been cut in the rock but take care for they can be slippery if wet. The steps end at a small platform overlooking the waves. Above and to the right (N) a cleft in the rocks marks the site of St. Mary's Well.

Like all good Welsh wells it has magic associated with it. Despite being lashed by the saltwater waves the well always provides fresh water from the cleft. The trip across the rocks to test this phenomenon is not desperately difficult, but is a scramble and would not be suitable for young children or anyone unsteady on their feet. There is a legend that if a finger is dipped in the well, and the person then keeps silent until the finger is perfectly dry, the wish (presumably a silent one) will be granted. Such stories are useful for the leaders of large noisy parties!

Some authorities state that pilgrims for Bardsey embarked from this spot. It is the nearest mainland point to the island, which looks quite close from here. The sound between the mainland and Bardsey is however notorious for its swift and dangerous currents, and to navigate into this rocky shore to pick up pilgrims seems to be hazardous. That is not to say that no one ever set off from this point but by far the most famous starting point for the trip is a bay much nearer Aberdaron.

The ascent of Mynydd Mawr is also recommended. There is a concrete road to the top of the hill but also various tracks through the gorse and heather. The views from the top are excellent, especially of Bardsey Island. A stroll down towards the sea on the north side opens up good views of the cliffs, and also demonstrates the strength of the currents hereabouts. The swirling eddies and whirlpools show the dangers of these waters.

As for the main route the time has now come to turn round and begin the journey away from Bardsey. The South Coast of the Lleyn is as delightful in its own way as the North Coast, and while evidence of the passage of pilgrims is less easy to find, there are many sites of historical interest, and some beautiful scenery. However to end the chapter at civilisation it is necessary to walk the couple of miles into Aberdaron.

At first sight there seem to be a number of tracks leading across the hillside in the right direction towards the headland to the south. These tracks however only flatter to deceive because there is no legitimate exit from the headland to reach the cliff path which takes you into Aberdaron. It is therefore necessary to retrace your steps back to the road which led to the end of the peninsula. Despite this lack of direct access the section to Aberdaron is extremely fine with excellent coastal scenery for most of its length.

Walk north-east back along the road for 150 yards until the first house on the right is passed, called Ty Mawr. Just after this is a corrugated iron barn and then two gates on the right leading onto a wide track. At the gates is a maker with the word "Gwyddel" (see photograph p82). This track soon leads to another gate, after which the track splits. Take the left-hand branch

Bardsey Island - the objective of pilgrims through the ages

(virtually straight on) to reach a gate by some corrugated barns. Pass through and bear slightly right to a gate and stile displaying a Celtic cross waymark. Over the stile bear left diagonally across the corner of the field to a further gate and stile, again with a Celtic cross. Over the stile walk alongside the fence on the left for a few yards to a gate and waymark giving access to a green lane.

Follow the green lane until it emerges on to a road. To the left is a large swampy area with a pond. Cyclists and walkers have been together over this section, but now they part company, cyclists turning left past the pond and walkers turning right.

Walk along the road until the tarmac disappears and degenerates into two unmade tracks. Take the left-hand of these (SE) along a green lane to a gate. Go through the gate and carry straight on along the line of the fence which is atop a bank. (Ignore the stile near the gate which leads off to the left.) Soon a stile is reached at a fence junction. Go over and carry on in the same direction by the bank which now has a drystone wall on it. Soon a gate

*After visiting the very tip of the peninsula this track is the start of
the way back along the south coast of the Lleyn*

is reached at a wall junction with a signpost to Mynydd Mawr and Porth
Meudy. Pass through the gate and walk alongside a fence on the right to a
stile and gate. Turn right over the stile and then walk up the little hill to
the top where there is a cairn. This is a good viewpoint.

On arriving at the cairn turn left and follow the track down the hillside
(E). Take care in this area for the tracks are somewhat indeterminate and
there are several of them. The hillside drops to the top of a line of cliffs and
the way trends left (NE), still on poor tracks. This is not shown as a right
of way on the map but is National Trust property so still perfectly legal.
Whichever faint track has been chosen by heading along the cliff top the
track soon improves and becomes very plain. Soon a stile is reached and
below at the water's edge can be seen some disused harbour facilities. Keep
walking the track along the cliff top, ignoring stiles which provide access
to roads inland. After about a mile steps lead down to a narrow cove.

This is Porth Meudy and a stream flows along the valley into the
sea. A couple of boats are usually moored here together with lobster
pots and fishing tackle. There is a signpost to Pen y Cil and
Aberdaron. Porth Meudy is traditionally the place where pilgrims

The impressive cliffs at the 'Land's End' of Wales

embarked for the last, and most dangerous, stage of the trip to Bardsey. This is therefore one of the few places along the route where the modern day traveller can say with certainty that they are standing exactly on the Pilgrims Route. Those who wish to emulate the pilgrims and complete the trip to Bardsey can take heart from a notice nearby which cites Mr. Evans (Tel: 01758 730654) as being willing to arrange the trip. It is to be hoped that Mr. Evans has a modern boat for this description of the passage appears in the *Ward Lock Red Guide to Wales* of 1919:

"Visitors who desire to make the journey to Bardsey Island should have plenty of time on their hands. In the first place it may be necessary to wait for days at Aberdaron before a favourable combination of wind and tide permits the passage to be made; and in the second, should the weather be unsettled, a sudden change may render return impossible for a considerable period."

Having lost all the height you must now regain it by a series of steps on the other side of the cove. The track then continues much as before along the cliff top. Soon the track splits at a signpost marked Aberdaron and Porth Meudy. Take the right-hand track down the steps to reach first the boulders of the shore and then the beach at Aberdaron itself and the end of the short promenade. This leads into the centre of the town.

Aberdaron village. The last staging post on the Pilgrims' Route before the hazardous sea trip to Bardsey

CYCLISTS

So far on this route it has been possible to avoid an excess of tarmac, but the section between Nefyn and Aberdaron is not as well endowed with cycling rights of way as the previous sections. It is possible by moving inland to pick up bridleways but to stay near the coast you have to use country lanes.

In this section a balance is attempted between sorties away from the coast and the lanes themselves. Those armed with the 1:25,000 OS map can amend that balance to suit personal preference. Riders should note that the lane which parallels much of the North Coast in this area is very quiet, and serves a few isolated hamlets. The main road runs a mile inland and takes the major traffic flow. The route along the lanes is enjoyable in its own right.

On arrival in Nefyn cycle into the town to the main road

junction. The turn to the right leads to Morfa Nefyn and Porth Dinllaen, which are well worth a visit. (See circular walk (a) below). The main route goes south-west at this point following the A497 to reach a roundabout (OS Ref: 297394) in 1 1/2 miles. Go straight on at the roundabout travelling south-west on a quiet lane. Pass the crossroads at Glanrhyd (OS Ref: 283384).

A right turn here leads to the village of Edern (1 mile) which was one of the main stopping places on the Pilgrims Route to Bardsey. Edern, according to some writers, was the son of Beli ab Maelgwyn Gwynedd who was king in this area. Beli was succeeded by another of his sons Iago who was therefore the brother of Edern. Iago died in 613 so Edern must have been one of the earliest saints of the area.

The main route carries straight on to the south-west and soon arrives at the farm of Cefn Leisiog (OS Ref: 271375). Turn left at the farm. The correct gate is the one before the main farm entrance passing the left (E) side of the house. The farm is at the top of a gentle rise in the road, but unfortunately the name of the farm is only on the main gate. This may mean that a 30 yard backtrack will be made to find the correct gate. Pass through the gate and in 20 yards come into a field. The correct line hugs the hedgeline on the right-hand side of the field.

This route is shown as a RUPP on the OS map, so there is every legal right to cycle it. However the farmer at Cefn Leisiog is not totally convinced, although he admits that there is a right of way. He is a lot happier if bikes are wheeled down the field, and whilst legally speaking this is a nonsense, it may be the best way to keep everybody happy.

At the bottom of the field is a stile and a small bridge over a drainage gully. Once over the bridge cross the field bearing slightly right to a gate leading into a green lane. Cycle up the green lane past the farm on the right and soon the lane upgrades and tarmac appears. In 50 yards a small church appears on the left in a grove of trees.

This is Llandudwen church, dedicated to St. Tudwen, one of the few female saints to achieve fame in this area. She is supposed to have founded the original church in the middle of the 5th century, which is very early indeed. If this were so it would be reasonable to assume that the Bardsey pilgrims would have known of it, yet it is

The interior of Llandudwen church. The church is 'T' shaped, because after part of it fell down it was considered too expensive to restore to its former glory.

not one of the churches mentioned on the pilgrim's way. Nevertheless it is a pleasant spot and well worth a visit.

The church is an odd shape, being in the form of a 'T'. Apparently it was built in the normal cross shape but the eastern arm of the cross collapsed. The community could not afford the cost of rebuilding the whole structure and so built a wall straight across to save money. On entering the church the font is seen on the right. The font is over a thousand years old and is carved from a piece of granite.

On the way out of the church grounds can be found a large boulder just by the entrance gate. Legend has it that this is a Druid "Stone of Testimony". This was used to settle disputes among local people for any agreement arrived at over the stone was binding on all parties. It seems that there is a curse on the stone which states that anyone who tries to remove it would be executed. Exactly what happens now that capital punishment has been abolished is unclear! In later years it was used as a mounting block for those attending church on horses.

From the church continue along the lane to a road junction. Turn

Cycling route at Brynodol Farm, heading towards Tudweiliog

right. Cycle the lane and take the second turning right at Dinas church (OS Ref: 269361) to reach a crossroads. Go straight on. In $^1/_2$ mile the road turns sharp left and then in 250 yards a bridleway appears on the right (OS Ref: 254362). The bridleway appears somewhat overgrown, but apart from a couple of low branches is easy enough. After 200 yards a gate appears and a track junction. Bear slightly right and along the track with the large impressive house on the left (see photograph). The track is plain but abruptly finishes at a gate into a field. The line goes straight across the field, and a faint trackline can be seen which leads to another gate. Through the gate the green lane reappears and should be followed to reach the road. Turn left towards Tudweiliog. The village provides accommodation and shops. The route however turns right just before the village onto a narrow lane signposted to the beach (OS Ref: 239372).

This lane now follows the coastline via Porthysgaden (OS Ref: 226371) and Tyddyn Sander (OS Ref: 221364) to reach a crossroads at Pont Pen-y-graig (OS Ref: 203333). Along this stretch there are signed opportunities to walk down to the sea, and view the fine coastal scenery. At the crossroads go right and left in 100 yards and stay on this lane ignoring all turn-offs to reach the 'T' junction at Ty Hen (OS Ref: 178310). Cyclists and walkers are together here. Turn right then bear left at the next junction. (Bearing right at this point leads to Porth Iago, a highly recommended diversion described in the walkers' section.)

In $1/2$ mile a track goes off to the right marked by a double gate and two large cylindrical concrete gateposts. The track is a good green lane to start but degenerates eventually and leads down to Porth Oer, the Whistling Sands. It is not clear if bicycles have the right to travel along beaches, but given the damage sand can do to bearings it is perhaps best to walk your machine the length of the beach. At the southern end of the beach is a small cafe and cyclists must pedal up the lane by its side to rejoin the road, when a right turn is made. Cycle along the road for 200 yards until a gate is seen on the right just before the road itself bends to the left. Go through the gate and cycle the unmade track, always bearing left to circumvent the hill of Mynydd Carreg (OS Ref: 164293). The track is wide and obvious and loops round the base of the hill to rejoin the road. Turn right. Eagle-eyed mapreaders will realise that only 300 yards has been gained since leaving the road, as the track completes almost a full circle. It does however provide a pleasant interlude from the recent preoccupation with tarmac.

In $1/2$ mile a 'T' junction is reached by a chapel and a phone box (OS Ref: 163284). Turn right. Follow this lane, which curves around the lower slopes of Mynydd Anelog, to arrive at a crossroads at Pont Afon Saint (OS Ref: 166267). Turn right here and follow this road to the south-west, ignoring all side lanes, until the road finishes in the car park at the end of the peninsula. To visit the cliffs at the end of the Lleyn and to see St. Mary's Well it will be necessary to padlock the bike and proceed as described in the walking section above. This is the furthest point of the peninsula and the return trip along the South Coast must now be started.

Retrace the way along the road for 150 yards to the first house on the right. Just after this a gate on the right gives access to an orange coloured bridleway. This leads to another gate, after which the track splits. Take the left-hand branch (virtually straight on) to reach a gate by some corrugated barns. Pass through and bear slightly right to a gate and stile displaying a Celtic cross waymark. Over the stile bear left diagonally across the corner of the field to a further gate and stile, again with a Celtic cross. Over the stile cycle alongside the fence on the left for a few yards to a gate and waymark giving access to a green lane. Follow the green lane until it emerges on to a road.

To the left is a large swampy area with much vegetation. Cyclists and walkers have been together over this section, but now they part company, cyclists bearing left past the swamp and walkers turning right. Turn left alongside the swamp area and continue for 200 yards when a turn should be made left into another narrow lane. Continue for 500 yards when an unmade lane on the right shows the way. (If you reach a sharp left-hand bend in the road you have gone 50 yards too far.) Take the muddy green lane until it meets tarmac again. Bear left and follow this road to a 'T' junction and turn right. At the crossroads shortly afterwards (Pont Afon-Saint) turn right and thence down the hill into Aberdaron.

OTHER WALKS IN THIS AREA

a) Morfa Nefyn and Port Dinllaen

Start:	Linksway Hotel, Morfa Nefyn
Car park:	Ample at roadside, also bus service from Nefyn
OS Ref:	283406
Distance:	3 miles
Ascent:	Negligible
Grade:	C

This is merely a sampling of the main route but is such a delightful stretch that it is worth doing in its own right. Start at the large Linksway Hotel on the west side of Morfa Nefyn. Walk up the lane towards the golf club and then follow directions as for the main route. Having walked around the headland of Porth Dinllaen, where the main route heads off south-west along the coast, cut back along an obvious track past some huts to get back to the clubhouse and thus return to Morfa Nefyn.

b) The cliffs of Aberdaron

Start:	Aberdaron village
Car park:	Ample in village, also infrequent bus connections
OS Ref:	174264
Distance:	3 miles
Ascent:	330ft
Grade:	C

This route also samples part of the main route. Start from Aberdaron and walk west along the beach to the end of the bay. A track then climbs up to the right using steps to gain the cliff tops. A signpost points the way to Porth Meudy. Turn left at the signpost and follow the well trodden path along the cliff top. There are excellent views of the wild sea cliffs of this final part of the peninsula, but also excellent views back towards Aberdaron. After about a mile steps lead down to the narrow cove of Porth Meudy where there is a slipway and a river coming down the valley. Thus far the walk has followed the main route in reverse.

Turn inland and follow the track up the narrow valley which branches after some 500 yards. Take the bridleway along the right-hand branch (N) to emerge at a lane. Turn right. Follow the lane to a 'T' junction and then turn right. A crossroads is soon reached where you turn right again. A few yards down the road a track leaves on the right and should be taken. After passing a house on the right and an old summerhouse on the left, keep left when the track branches, past another house to rejoin the road. A right turn leads down the hill back into Aberdaron.

c) Carn Fadryn

Start:	Garnfadryn village
Car park:	Parking very limited
OS Ref:	277346
Distance:	2½ miles
Ascent:	700ft
Grade:	B (a short walk but steep in places)

Although this hill is not part of the coastal route itself it is well worth a visit, not only for the commanding views of the south-west end of the peninsula but also for its historical interest. Carn Fadryn (sometimes Fadrun) rises to a height of 1218ft. It is an excellent specimen of an Iron Age fort and there are signs of fortifications from different eras. There are two lines of defensive walls, the inner one enclosing an area of some 12 acres. There are traces of circular huts inside the inner defensive wall, but also considerable remains outside the defences at the base of the hill to the north-west. Those who have visited the remains at Tre'r Ceiri above Trefor will be disappointed, for the remains on Carn Fadryn are nothing like as well preserved. However for views of the Lleyn, Carn Fadryn is difficult to beat.

The summit is reached from the little hamlet of Garnfadryn 5 miles due south of Morfa Nefyn. The road junction at the start of the walk is marked by a phone box and a chapel. Walk north up the little lane by the side of the little house next to the chapel to reach open country at a gate. Go through the gate and turn immediately right (E) along a well defined track. The track soon starts to climb and veers round to the left through bracken, and follows the line of a drystone wall. The path then bears left again and steepens as it makes for the summit. The track remains very obvious as it zigzags up the hillside, and there are cairns at regular intervals. The summit with its trig pillar is soon reached.

There are some remains of hut circles just below the summit to the north-east but you will need to use your imagination a little. The traces are there if you look hard enough. The view needs no imagination and is magnificent. The whole of the southern end of the Lleyn peninsula is laid out, with excellent views of Rhiw mountain and the bays of the coast. Looking east is a vista of mountains ranging from Yr Eifl, through the main Snowdonian massif, round to the Rhinogs to the south-east.

The view across the bay at Aberdaron

CHAPTER 5
Aberdaron to Abersoch

Aberdaron today is a small, pleasant village well served by hotels, guesthouses and cafes. It was not always like this and in fact only the advent of the motor car has opened up the village to tourists. Many of the resorts of the Lleyn were served by the railways which were developed in the 19th century, but the line never reached as far as Aberdaron, despite its title as "The Land's End of Wales".

Thomas Pennant, a prolific writer and traveller through Wales in the 18th century, merely describes it as a "poor village". Even one hundred years later the village scarce gets a mention in the Guide to Wales of 1878. However by 1919 the Red Guide to Wales described Aberdaron as "the remotest and quaintest village on the Lleyn", and noted that a motor bus ran twice daily from Pwllheli.

Despite Pennant's remarks the area has a history going back into the mists of time. Just 2 miles north-east of the village is Castell Odo (OS Ref: 187285). This hill, rising to nearly 500ft, was the site of the earliest Iron Age settlement in North Wales. The earliest inhabitants constructed wooden huts and a palisade for defence, and there are traces of 10 circular huts. Various pieces of pottery have been found at the site, the oldest dating from 425 BC.

We can surmise that the village was still popular in the 6th century AD. for it marked the final stage of the Pilgrims Route. It was the last holy site before reaching Bardsey, and the church was important in its own right. It is likely that there has been a building on this site since the 6th century, but the present day church is a mixture of various architectural eras. There is a late Norman door of the 12th century, and the north nave dates from the same period. The church was enlarged in the 15th century by the addition of the south nave. The church fell into disrepair in the mid 19th century, but was renovated before the ravages of time did too much damage.

The church is jointly dedicated to St. Lleuddad, the second abbot of Bardsey and St. Hywyn (or Henwyn). The latter arrived from Brittany in the 6th century, and was one of the first saints of Bardsey.

*The church at Aberdaron. The church is jointly dedicated to St. Lleuddad,
the second abbot of Bardsey, and St. Hywyn who arrived on Bardsey
from Brittany in the 6th century*

He was reputed to be a cousin of St. Cadfan, the first abbot of
Bardsey, and related to St. Maelrhys, of whom more later. In later
times the church was used as a place of sanctuary. In 1095 Gruffudd
ap Cynan escaped from the Normans at Chester and arrived at
Aberdaron where the church elders hid him and later got him on a
boat to escape to Ireland.

Gruffudd must have made his peace with the Normans for the
next time he is involved with a sanctuary problem the roles are
reversed. In 1115 Gruffudd ap Rhys, a prince from South Wales, fled
to escape the treachery of the original Gruffudd ap Cynan who
proposed to deliver the young prince into the clutches of King
Henry I. The prince sought sanctuary in Aberdaron church, but
orders were given for him to be forcibly removed. The local clergy
then made such a fuss at this proposed violation that the soldiers
would not carry out their orders. Under cover of darkness the
young prince escaped by boat back to South Wales.

The oddest inhabitant of Aberdaron seems to have been one

"Dick of Aberdaron", sometimes spelt "Dic". Dick's full name was Richard Robert Jones who was born some time in the 1780s. Despite being from peasant stock Dick had a remarkable talent for learning languages and eventually was able to use upwards of 15 different tongues. Such talent was hardly needed in Aberdaron at the time and Dick drifted along the North Wales coast, eventually arriving in Liverpool. Here he could converse with foreign sailors, but his skills never seemed to provide him with a sufficient income.

He appears to have been something of an eccentric, wandering around in unusual baggy clothing, and according to some writers sporting a French horn around his neck which he used to attract attention before addressing the crowds in some unknown dialect. He died around 1844 and is buried in the churchyard at St. Asaph.

Considering the great number and diversity of paths west of Aberdaron it is somewhat disappointing to discover that the paths to the east are much more restricted. There is no right of way along the cliff edge, and a way must be found inland, with occasional forays to the sea. Nevertheless a continuous route is available and has some very good sections. Unfortunately the most difficult part of the next section is the start. The route from Aberdaron lies along the attractive Daron Valley which runs just north of east from the town.

Until 1995 the access to the valley was straightforward, although it varied a little from the official right of way. The opening of a new caravan site has closed off this simple connection and the "official" right of way is overgrown to the point of being almost impassable. This state of affairs is being dealt with but if a blockage is found at this point the best alternative is to take the road leading east from the village past the old church.

From the bridge in the centre of Aberdaron walk north and then first right along the B4413 road. Ahead it climbs steeply and the OS map indicates that a right of way leaves the road on the right about 100 yards from the junction over a low wall. In fact two stone steps appear next to a telegraph pole. A profusion of brambles does not assist but a narrow way through can be found. Over the stone steps the line then bears left and contours the hillside above a small caravan site. The vegetation is considerable, so that whilst the track is usually passable in May it is well blocked by September.

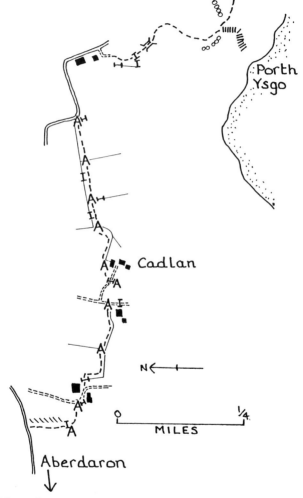

Porth Ysgo

Cadlan

N ←——|

0   1/4
         MILES

Aberdaron

Aberdaron to Porth Ysgo
Sketchmap 5.1

The beach at Porth Ysgo
Hell's Mouth from Rhiw

The "Cat Rock" at Porth Ceiriad
Abersoch

Soon a fence is reached (missing stile) which is clambered over to gain the river meadows. The problems are now over as a faint track appears. The navigation is easy for the route stays in the valley bottom heading east-north-east.

After a pleasant ¹/₂ mile a crossing of the river must be made. The place is not too obvious, but there are some landmarks. First the track starts to trend left and if followed leads to a stile. If this point is reached retrace steps back to the river. The point of crossing is 60 yards below a large tree trunk slung across the river with a gate hanging from it into the water.

Cross the river on boulders onto the bank. Just above, a double hedgeline forms a little green lane leading to a gate. Pass through the gate and walk alongside the fence up the field to reach a junction with three gates at Morfa Farm (OS Ref: 183265). Turn left along the road. This point can also be reached direct from Aberdaron along the road by the church.

Keen mapreaders will notice a right of way continuing straight on at this point which appears to have the possibility of looping round to meet this same lane higher up. You are welcome to try but on both occasions when the author has tried this route the main field has contained a rather frisky bull. Discretion being the better part of valour...

Walk along the lane for almost a mile until a footpath is marked on the right with a signpost saying "Porth Cadlan 1¹/₂ miles" (sketchmap 5.1). Take the path and walk alongside a grassy bank to a gate and a stile. Over the stile turn left along a sunken lane through gorse to reach another stile giving access to a farm lane. Ignore the turns in the lane and carry on in the same direction to walk across the front of the farmhouse to a gate. Through the gate turn right and follow the field boundary which soon turns left to reach a stile.

Stay on the same line along the next field boundary, passing a telegraph pole, and a house on the other side of the fence to the right. Soon you can go no further, but there is a stone stile as part of the wall, somewhat overgrown, but a little searching will soon locate it. Drop onto a farm track.

Turn left but in 5 yards turn right along another farm track which drops gently to a gate. Continue on the track through the gate. There are now some buildings in front, but the correct line passes behind them. Leave the track as the buildings are reached to find a stile on the left and a track leading behind the left-hand building. Turn right over the stile but then trend left alongside the fence until another stile is reached.

The farm buildings to the right are called Cadlan Isaf, and a detour can be made to the sea at Porth Cadlan. The site has historical connections for there is one theory that King Arthur's last battle against his arch enemy Mordred was fought in the fields around Porth Cadlan. It has to be said that one can find the supposed traces of King Arthur's last battle at a number of sites around the western seaboard of England and Wales. However, this area does have some evidence to connect it with Arthur.

First, Arthur's last battle was the battle of Camlan. This name is a derivative of an old Welsh word *Cadgamlan* meaning "rout". The word can also be shortened to Cadlan. Secondly, the word Cadlan is taken by some to mean "battle site". Finally, there is a large rock just offshore at Porth Cadlan called Maen Gwenonwy which means Gwenonwy's stone. Gwenonwy was the sister of King Arthur.

Of more interest are the connections between Arthur and the saints of the Lleyn. Gwenonwy was married to Gwyndaf Hen and one of their children was Hywyn, the saint dedicated to Aberdaron church. So King Arthur was Hywyn's uncle. Now Gwyndaf Hen had a brother, Gwyddno, and a sister Gwen Teirbron. Gwyddno had a son called Maelrhys, an early saint on Bardsey. His church is a little way to the east and is described later. Gwen Teirbron married Eneas Lydewig and their son was Cadfan who as we already know was the first abbot of Bardsey. Thus Cadfan, Maelrhys and Hywyn were all cousins. All clear now?

Go over the stile and keep straight on with the fenceline on the left. Three more stiles bring the route onto a narrow lane. Turn right. The lane jinks to the left and later to the right but soon a large pond is seen on the left, and barns on the right. In 50 yards a sign is reached, "Footpath to Porth Ysgo". Turn right along an obvious track (see photograph). This leads alongside a barn to a gate. Do NOT go through the gate but turn left at it alongside a fence to reach two gates side by side.

Pass through the smaller gate and drop down to a bridge over a stream. The track which is very plain leads down a delightful little valley to reach some steps, and waymarks.

At this point it is possible to stay high and contour round the headland to reach more steps leading away from the beach up a small valley. However a descent to the beach is recommended. Walk down the steps - a considerable number of them - to reach the beach below.

The route down to the delightful Porth Ysgo is designated only as a footpath, however cyclists are compensated a little by taking the lane which passes Llanfaelrhys church.

This is Porth Ysgo and a prettier cove you could not hope to find. At the point where the steps reach the beach a waterfall comes over the cliff just to add a little extra to the scenery. The beach is firm fine sand and, facing due south, is a veritable sun trap. The only drawback is that all those steps have to be climbed to get back on route. Never mind, the views are worth it!

Climb up the steps but now keep right and into the little valley of Nant Gadwen (OS Ref: 212266) on an easy track. Follow the stream uphill, passing some small mine workings on the right, to arrive at a road by a huge wild fuscia bush. The mines date from the mid 19th century when a considerable amount of manganese ore was excavated. The mines ceased production in 1945. At the road junction the correct route turns very sharp right (S). If time permits a slight detour to the left can be made to visit the church of St. Maelrhys, as described below.

It has been noted previously that there is more evidence of pilgrim relics on the North Coast of the Lleyn than the south. The South Coast has no designated line of churches, at least as far as we know. Some writers dismiss the South Coast route, but most admit

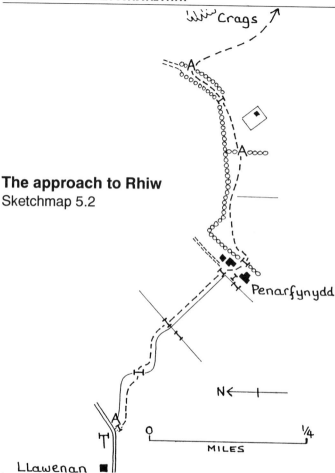

The approach to Rhiw

Sketchmap 5.2

that there must have been some travellers who approached this way. One explanation is that pilgrims took a boat from the Barmouth area to arrive at Pwllheli. This was to avoid the problematic river crossings at Portmadoc. This method of completing a pilgrimage does seem to be cheating a little!

One site which could have been a South Coast stopping place is the church of St. Maelrhys at Llanfaelrhys. To visit the church turn left at the junction and walk along the lane for 400 yards when the church is seen on the right. This is the only site dedicated to St. Maelrhys in the British Isles but he was one of the original band of saints who were contemporaries of St. Cadfan, and therefore of some importance. The relationship between Maelrhys and Cadfan has already been described.

On the boundary between Llanfaelrhys and Rhiw parishes are two large stones. One stands on its end, but the other appears to have fallen over. Legend is that two thieves broke into St. Maelrhys' church and stole whatever money they could find. They then escaped towards Rhiw but just as they crossed the parish boundary they were turned into two granite columns for their sacrilege. The stones are called Llandron Maelrhys (Maelrhys' thieves) to this day.

Back on the main route, having turned sharp right at the junction, follow the lane for 400 yards passing the entrance to the farm at Llawenan (OS Ref: 214268). Soon a track is seen on the right, with a gate and a stile (sketchmap 5.2). The turn-off is just after some telegraph wires cross the road. Over the stile keep left alongside the fence to a gate. Pass through, still keeping by the fence which is now on the right. The fence curves round to the right and the track stays with it to reach a gate. Keep straight on to another gate at a farm road.

This is the farm of Penarfynydd (OS Ref: 219267). Go through the gate and bear half right to pass between the house and outbuildings. Above is a drystone wall with a gate. Through the gate turn left and walk alongside the wall. The path trends away from the wall slightly and gains height to reach a stile. Over the stile stay by the wall passing a pen marked "Danger" to reach a gate giving access to a green lane.

Walk up the green lane but soon take a stile on the right over the wall. A track heads off across the heathland. Above and to the left is a rocky outcrop (see sketchmap 5.2) and soon a faint track cuts off left towards the rocks. This should be ignored, but it forms part of circular walk (a) at the end of this chapter. Press on along the main track heading towards the sea. Soon the route passes some broken walls and crests a rise from where there are fine views of the cliffs in this area.

The OS map does not show any rights of way around this headland but the land is owned by the National Trust and the path is plain to see. The area is rich in remains and the OS map notes several 'hut circles' and 'standing stones'. One circle can be seen by the ruin of the cottage at Pen-yr-ogof (OS Ref: 232274). Another rich site is the field to the right just as the track approaches the houses at Rhiw where there are the remains of round huts, field terraces and enclosures.

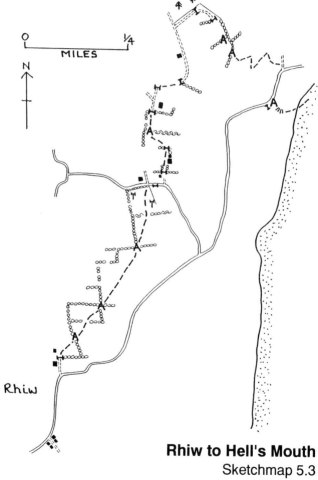

Rhiw to Hell's Mouth
Sketchmap 5.3

The path stays high above the waves on the headland and is a very pleasant section of walking. Eventually a gate at a drystone wall is reached. Pass through the gate and stay alongside the wall to another gate giving access to an unmade lane. Signs of civilisation are now beginning to appear as the village of Rhiw is reached. Stay on the unmade lane until a road appears (sketchmap 5.3).

Turn right along the road (ignoring the footpath sign opposite) and continue along it for 200 yards where it takes a sharp turn to the right. At this point an unmade lane goes straight on just below a large white house. Take the unmade lane to a gate and pass through. There is a ruined barn on the left. Trend right through nettles to reach a stone stile in the wall.

Over the stile bear left to go through a gap in a wall. Keep on the same line to drop to the other side of the field where the wall junction seems to present an obstacle. As you get closer an old stone stile is seen through the weeds giving access to the next field, down and to the right. Cross this field diagonally right to reach the opposite wall at the point where the wall comes in from the more distant fields. Again an old stone stile is found.

Its use allows you to walk along the top of the broad wall. This is necessary because to the left is an uninviting bog, and to the right brambles. After a couple of yards drop off to the right and continue diagonally across the fields. Pass a broken wall and go past a telegraph pole to reach the corner of the field. Unlike the last few walls there is no stile here ancient or otherwise, but 20ft to the left the wall is broken down and allows access to a road. Turn right.

Walk for 100 yards down the road until it turns right. At this point a good track leads off to the left and should be taken. Along the track there are excellent views to the right, and soon an old garage is reached by a gate. Go through the gate into a green lane and a building on the left, but as the building comes level bear left slightly by a ramp to go past a telegraph pole onto a sunken track. Go left along the sunken track to the first wall, and turn right below it. Keep alongside the wall to a stile. The choice of route in this area is limited by the profusion of gorse.

Over the stile keep straight on to reach a gate and then a deserted farm on the right. The way lies straight on ignoring a branch to the left to reach another gate at a 'T' junction. Turn right along the wide track, going through a further gate before the track swings to the left and passes a little cottage.

Soon a track junction is reached by the start of a forest. Turn right.

Follow the track on the forest's edge through a gate as it swings right and becomes narrower. Another gate soon leads to a stone stile, but keep straight on by the side of the forest. Soon the trees fall back and shortly after a stone stile appears in the wall on the left and a waymark is seen. Go over this stile onto a plain track which now zigzags down the hillside, quite steeply in places, to reach a cart track at the bottom. Turn right to reach a road in 20 yards.

Turn right along the road for 50 yards to the point where it sweeps right. Here a stile is found on the left giving obvious access to the beach below. There is a campsite 100 yards past the stile along the road at Treheli Farm. The stile leads onto a track which soon loses height. However the last few yards to the beach are so steep that steps have been constructed. The winter gales obviously wreak havoc on the steps for it is obvious that their line has been changed over the years. Soon the beach is reached.

This is Hell's Mouth. Inland from Hell's Mouth is an area of flat ill-drained farmland. The bay must have been much larger at one time, but remains of the Ice Age in the form of a thick layer of boulder clay has filled in much of the bay leaving the shoreline at its present point. The landscape thus formed inland is flat and uninteresting and not particularly well endowed with rights of way. Our route has not stayed on the shoreline previously for more than a matter of yards, but along this South Coast there are places where it is the best option. Therefore the route now leads along the sands right around the bay. Well, it is supposed to be a Coastal Walk!

The Welsh name for the bay is Porth Neigwl, but it is commonly called Hell's Mouth. The name dates from the days of sail when this part of the coast had a terrible reputation for wrecks. A combination of south-westerly gales and some treacherous offshore currents spelled the doom of several sailing ships. In gale conditions it is still an awesome place.

The walk around the bay will take an hour or so, but there are good views of the cliffs of boulder clay which, being soft, are continually attacked by the sea. There are dire warnings at regular intervals of the folly of getting too close or trying to climb them.

Towards the end of the bay the cliffs get lower and as rocky outcrops begin to appear in the sand cut left onto the top of the low cliffs. Nant Farm can be seen (OS Ref: 294256), and the map indicates a number of rights of

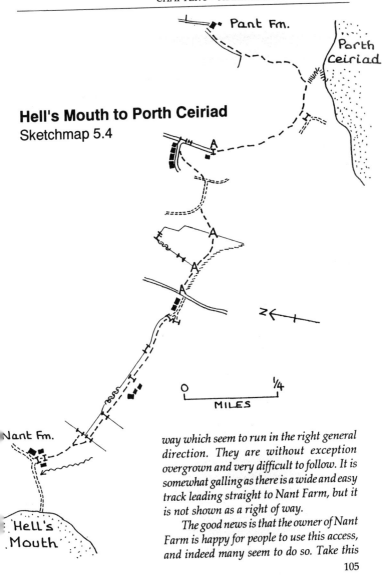

Hell's Mouth to Porth Ceiriad

Sketchmap 5.4

way which seem to run in the right general direction. They are without exception overgrown and very difficult to follow. It is somewhat galling as there is a wide and easy track leading straight to Nant Farm, but it is not shown as a right of way.

The good news is that the owner of Nant Farm is happy for people to use this access, and indeed many seem to do so. Take this

105

track to reach Nant Farm (sketchmap 5.4 p105), then turn right just before the farmhouse to cut across the farmyard, entering by one gate and leaving by a gate opposite. From here a track climbs up the hill with a small valley on the right.

It is also possible from Nant Farm to divert along tracks to the north to reach the village of Llanengan and by following the road for a mile and a half further north to arrive at Llangian. Both villages can claim some connection with the Bardsey pilgrims. The pretty village of Llangian has a unique burial pillar of late 5th century origin in its churchyard. The church at Llanengan has bells which are supposed to have come from the abbey on Bardsey. The villages are described more fully in the cyclists' section below.

The climb up the hill soon eases and two gates appear in a fence. Take the right-hand gate and keep by the fence on the left, passing through two more gates where the track widens to become a farm road just after some barns. Keep on this track to pass some bungalows on the left by a road junction. Dead ahead is a stile. Go over and stay by the grassy bank to another stile. Over this the bank curves away slightly right, and at this point the route curves about the same amount to the left to gain a stile over a fence. There is a black and white house to the left.

Over the stile keep on the track with bracken to the right and gorse to the left. The track drops onto an unmade lane where the route bears right. Ignore obvious tracks to left and right and keep straight on as the track narrows to go under some telephone wires. The path swings slightly right to a footpath sign and then left to reach a road by a house called Hafdy. Follow the road down to a 'T' junction and turn right.

Walk down the road for 200 yards where it ends at a caravan park called Nant y Big. A stile lies directly in front and leads into the head of a valley leading down to the sea. Walk downhill along a fence to an open cliff top where the path swings left along the fenceline. Soon a footpath sign is reached where a narrow track leads down to the beach at Porth Ceiriad. The route continues without necessarily dropping down to the beach but once again the diversion is worth the effort for this is a very picturesque spot with the fine cliffs of Trwyn yr Wylfa away to the east.

From the footpath sign showing the way to the beach turn inland (sketchmap 5.5) and climb the grassy hillside until fences coming in from both sides funnel the route to reach a gate. There is a caravan site to the left. Pass through the gate and follow the track to reach a lane by some barns

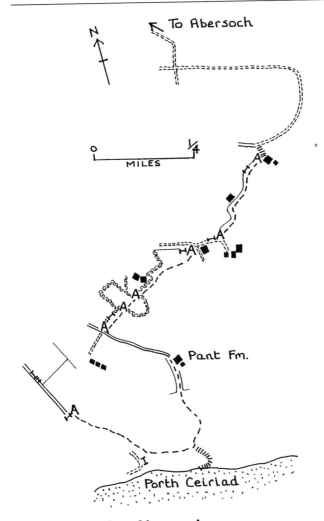

Porth Ceiriad to Abersoch
Sketchmap 5.5

with a campsite to the left. The barns form part of Pant Farm (OS Ref: 314254).

Walk up the lane (NW) for 100 yards until a cattle grid is reached. A stile on the right gives access to a field so keep by the left-hand fence and hedge, past a telegraph pole to a stile. Over the stile aim diagonally left to a gap in the hedge opposite which leads to a stile on the right over another hedge.

Over the stile turn left and walk along the track which stays close to the hedgeline but not slavishly so. Go past some cottages on the left and a telegraph pole to reach a stile by a gate in the top left corner of the meadow. Over the stile turn right along a farm track. The big house at Cim is now on the right and there is a caravan site on the left (OS Ref: 317257). Stay on the track as it curves right behind the big house and as barns come into view a gate appears on the left. Go through the gate and then immediately over a stile on the right.

Once over the stile turn left and stay close by the fence as it drops down the hill, zigzagging slightly. At the bottom corner of the hill a stile appears behind a house. Go over the stile and then left down some steps, virtually in the garden of the house, to drop onto an unmade lane. Turn right.

Drop down the lane which is loose and shaly and as the coastline gets close the lane turns to the left and soon a crossroads is met with a footpath sign. Turn right and drop down towards the sea passing a picnic site on the left, and a small car park. Another path junction is met and a left turn should be made. This track now leads easily across the golf course, past the clubhouse on the left to reach a road. Turn left, then right at the main road in 150 yards to drop into the centre of Abersoch.

CYCLISTS

The North Coast of the Lleyn provides some exciting cycling, especially over Yr Eifl, and the cycleway south of Caernarfon gives facilities which, as yet, are still too infrequent. The South Coast of the peninsula has few long stretches off road and bikers will find that they are cycling along lanes more often than not. Nevertheless these lanes are noted for their lack of traffic, and you are more likely to meet a tractor than a car, and there are some little gems of off road tracks to link the lanes. The whole coast is very pretty and passes through several interesting historical sites.

There are no bridleways leading east from Aberdaron and the

road must be taken. From the centre of the village go past the Gwesty Ship Hotel, turn left and carry on up the road past the church. In 2 miles a crossroads is reached at Siop Pen-y-caerau (OS Ref: 201272) by a post box. Turn right. Cycle along the lane with several tight bends past the few houses at Ysgo and then passing the church of Llanfaelrhys on the left. The church and its connections to the Bardsey pilgrims is described in the walkers' section above. Soon a road junction is met with a large fuscia bush on the right. This is the head of Nant Gadwen and if time allows it is worth padlocking the bike and strolling down the valley to the delightful cove of Porth Ysgo. The area is rich in legends of King Arthur, as described in the walkers' section.

Returning to the road junction turn right and follow the lane passing the farm of Llawenan (OS Ref: 214268) and continue along the lane as it swings left to the north-east. In $1/2$ mile arrive at a 'T' junction and turn right. Climb up the hill into Rhiw village until a lane goes off to the left signposted to Sarn. Turn left and pass the post office and in 200 yards the lane splits. Bear left and cycle for 200 yards, then as the lane curves gently left turn right up a steep little road heading up towards the wireless mast.

As the gradient eases a gate appears in front leading onto an unmade track. Go through the gate, and note a faint track bearing left, but a better track to the right. The better right-hand track is taken and provides a section of glorious high level biking. The land rises again and a second radio mast is seen. There is a trig point just to the left which affords good views of the northern side of the peninsula. At a point level with the radio mast the track splits. Take the left-hand route which stays level for a while then drops off the side of the mountain to give an exhilarating fast descent to a lane.

Despite the attractions of a fast descent it is worth stopping about half way down to see the remains of a Neolithic axe factory. The point is not easy to see, but as the track loses height it comes close to a rocky outcrop on the left. Here the track swings right, drops a little and swings left quite sharply. The track then swings right again, and the Neolithic site is on the apex of this right-hand bend.

At this point note a series of odd circular hollows on the left, the largest one being about 15 yards across. They are not easy to see from the track so stroll down the hill for a few yards and the centres of the hollows become more obvious. This marks the site of the Neolithic axe factory, the hollows representing simple opencast workings to access the best rock. The remains of the factory were only discovered in 1956, but it may date back as far as 3000 BC. It certainly was in use for several centuries and knives and axe heads of various sizes originating from this factory have been found over much of Wales and into the English borders.

Whether or not you stop to view the axe factory you arrive at the lane. Turn left. There is a distinct lack of suitable off road tracks for a while, but take care along this lane because it soon drops steeply to reach a 'T' junction. Turn right. Stay on this lane, ignoring all turn-offs for just over 2 miles when the outskirts of Botwnnog are reached by a road junction with a chapel on the left (OS Ref: 262308). Turn right onto the main road signed to "Llanbedrog and Pwllheli". Cycle for 150 yards then turn right down a minor lane signed to "Plas yn Rhiw".

Stay on this lane without deviation, passing the church at Llandegwning (OS Ref: 267301). The church has an unusual spire, being octagonal near the base but rising to a cone. Carry on to arrive at a main road junction. Turn left, signed to "Mynytho and Abersoch". Cycle along this road for almost a mile and take the first turn on the right, signed to Llangian. At the next road junction (OS Ref: 282299) bear left and continue along the road to reach the pretty little village of Llangian.

Plaques in the village show that Llangian has in the past won the "Best kept village in Wales" award, and it is easy to see why. There is a pleasant church dating from the 13th century, but in the churchyard there is a particular rarity.

This takes the form of a rough stone pillar about 4ft high with a Latin inscription: *Meli Medici/Fili Martini/Iacit* meaning "(The stone) of Melus the Doctor, son of Martinus, he lies (here)". The rarity value of the stone lies in the fact that it mentions the deceased's profession, the only early Christian grave in the whole of Britain to do so. The stone dates from the 5th or early 6th century.

Although the church at Llangian is 13th century, Melus' gravestone shows that there was a Christian community here or nearby around the time of the early Bardsey saints. One glance at the

The church at Llande-gwning. The spire is unusual in that at the base it is octagonal but rises to a cone.

landscape behind the bay of Hell's Mouth shows it to be a flat and swampy area comprising boulder clay. This would not be a good route for the pilgrims to cross. Assuming then that travellers would have stayed on the rather drier, slightly higher land they would have passed through Llangian to get round the back of the wetlands. How-ever it has to be said that this is supposition, and there is no other supporting evidence.

The church itself is dedicated to St. Cian who was a pupil of St. Peris, after whom Llanberis is named. There are only scant references to St. Cian in ancient documents. He was thought to be a warrior and a poet, but what he did to become a saint is a mystery. Legend has it that he was a soldier who returned from one of the Roman armies. The links between this soldier and the patron saint of Llangian are tenuous but widely believed.

From Llangian take the main road south, keeping left at the road junction at Bont Newydd (OS Ref: 294285) to reach the village of Llanengan.

Llanengan has an impressive parish church dating from the 15th century. The bells of the church have 17th century dates and are believed to have come from the abbey on Bardsey. It seems that

The church at Llanengan. The bells in the church are reputed to be the ones originally used in the Bardsey abbey.

Llanengan was traditionally associated with the abbey on Bardsey. Whether the association was started early enough for Llanengan to be a stopping place on the Pilgrims Route is difficult to say. One writer notes "..it was no doubt a point of call for Bardsey pilgrims", but substantial evidence is lacking.

Llanengan is dedicated to Einion of whom mention has previously been made at Llanwnda (Chapter 2). He was styled 'King' of the Lleyn in the early 6th century, and was a descendant of Cunedda Wledig, the founder of Gwynedd.

At the road junction turn left and immediately right by the house called Tyddyn Llan to climb steeply up the lane which soon swings to the left. Continue east to a road junction in ¹/₂ mile and turn right down the hill. In 250 yards a crossroads is met. Turn left and in 100 yards turn right off road onto a track (OS Ref: 304266) through Sarn Farm. Bear right through the farmyard then left following an obvious track.

Pass through a gate and soon join a lane but continue straight on to an offset crossroads. Turn left and drop down the sandy track which levels out onto the side of the golf course. Continue to a track junction and then bear left along the golf course and past the clubhouse. The track now develops a tarmac surface and emerges on a suburban road. Turn left and up to the main road. Turn right and drop down into the town of Abersoch.

OTHER WALKS IN THIS AREA

a) Mynydd y Graig

Start:	Village of Rhiw 300 yards east of the post office
Car park:	Opportunities in various places nearby, also on bus route
OS Ref:	228277
Distance:	3 miles
Ascent:	450ft
Grade:	B (short but indistinct track and steep)

This is an excellent walk, abounding in historical relics and fine seascapes. It ascends the summit of Mynydd y Graig which is just under 800ft high.

It starts from the main road in Rhiw by some cottages and 100 yards from the chapel. On the opposite side of the road is a footpath sign. The first part of the walk is the main route in reverse. Walk south between the cottages on a good track to a gate. Keep straight on alongside the drystone wall to another gate. Pass through and where the track splits bear right and gain height to a crest by some low cliffs. Continue on the obvious footpath passing the ruin at Pant-yr-ogof with its associated round hut (see main route for details) and follow the obvious track as it contours high above the sea.

The track eventually bears right round the end of the hill and approaches a stile in a drystone wall. At this point look to the right to find a narrow track turning off to the right and gaining height towards a rocky outcrop. Do not go over the stile but take the narrow track some way before it. The track becomes faint but the way lies upwards along the crest of the hill. The angle soon eases and then steepens briefly to reach the summit.

This is the site of an Iron Age hill fort. As with many such antiquities it is difficult to discern the outline of the fort. On the north-west side the site was not fortified as the cliffs form a natural barrier, but there is some walling at the top of a narrow gully. The north-east side has the remains of a wall which contours the hillside but it is in a bad state of repair. On the west end of the flat top are the remains of a couple of circular stone huts. The date of occupation of this fort is not known.

Continue along the crest of the hill and pick up a narrow track descending from the summit ridge to the north-east. The track is faint and the ground steep and stony, but height is soon lost and the better track on which the walk started is reached. Turn left to walk the 1/4 mile back to the starting point.

b) Circular Cycle ride at Rhiw

Start:	Rhiw village below the radio mast
Car park:	Opportunities in the village
OS Ref:	224281
Distance:	4 miles
Ascent:	350ft
Grade:	Easy cycling on good off road tracks and country lanes

The cycling fraternity has been largely excluded from these circulars due to the lack of suitable bridleways or other legal tracks. However at Rhiw there are a number of such tracks which enable the off road biker to enjoy a short ride.

The route follows the main cycle route from Rhiw. Thus from the post office cycle up the hill on the road to Sarn. At the junction keep left and watch for the right turn up the steep lane below the radio mast. The traverse of the hill and the Neolithic site on the northern side are described fully above in the cycling main section. Follow this past the Neolithic site to the lane. At this point the main route turns left, but to complete this ride turn right and follow the lane easily back to the start.

c) Porth Ceiriad

Start:	Pant Farm or Abersoch
Car park:	Field by Pant Farm (honesty box for fee)

OS Ref:	314254
Distance:	Pant Farm - 2 miles, Abersoch - 9 miles
Ascent:	Negligible
Grade:	C

This cove near Abersoch is included for those travellers who cannot resist a dip in the sea as part of a holiday. Given the recent reports on pollution of the sea the author has not personally tested the waters, but is assured by one who has that it is a good place for bathing.

The walk described here is short, starting from Pant Farm (OS Ref: 314254) but for those wanting a longer walk it could be done from Abersoch by reversing the main route through the golf course and across the fields to the north-east of Pant Farm (see sketchmap 5.5).

Walk past the side of Pant Farm to a track which follows the edge of a small caravan site. This soon opens up into the head of a small green valley which drops down towards the sea. Soon the cliff edge is reached with footpath signs. There is only one way down to the beach but it is well provided with steps. Once on the beach it is worth strolling to the west end of the bay into a more secluded cove. The rock strata in the cliff are wonderfully shown and the dips and curves are impressive.

Regain the cliff top and walk west along it for a while until a footpath sign points the way inland up a narrow valley called Nant-y-big. There are one or two path junctions off to the right but keep left at such points until a gate is reached by a stile. This leads into a narrow lane with a caravan site office on the left (W). Continue up the lane for 150 yards to see two gates on the right, one a normal farm gate, the other a pedestrian kissing gate (shown on sketchmap 5.5). Go through the gate into the field but bear to the right to meet the fenceline. Follow the fenceline up the field towards the big clump of bracken.

Just as you enter the bracken a path junction appears. Take the right-hand track to reach the side of the field by a fence. Turn left up the rise, with houses on the other side of the fence. Keep by the fence and in due course a stile appears on the right. Go over it onto a good track and turn left. The track leads down to a lane. If you started at

Pant Farm you should turn right here to walk the last 200 yards. If you commenced the walk in Abersoch the route lies straight on and is described in the main route section above.

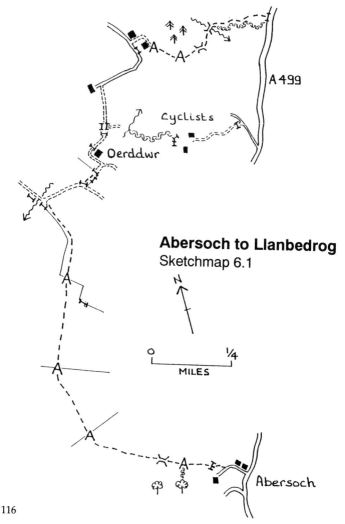

A 499

Cyclists

Oerddwr

Abersoch to Llanbedrog
Sketchmap 6.1

N

0   ¼
MILES

Abersoch

CHAPTER 6
Abersoch to Pwllheli

Abersoch is a famous seaside resort, particularly with the boating fraternity. The establishment of a good harbour added to its attractions for sailors, and there is a range of facilities catering for boating. The harbour is sheltered from the south-westerly gales that wreaked such havoc in earlier times at places like Hell's Mouth.

The harbour marks the mouth of the river, the Afon Soch, which follows a curious course to reach the sea. The river rises near Hell's Mouth but instead of draining direct to the sea it makes a huge loop to the north and then curves south through a gorge to reach Abersoch. The reason for this is that in the Ice Age a large glacial lake grew to the west, and as it eventually overflowed it cut the gorge as a deep channel. When the ice eventually melted the Afon Soch continued to use the line of the gorge to reach the sea..

Abersoch was not always so popular. The *Guide to Wales* of 1878 dismisses it in one line thus: ".. Abersoch (is) also near (to Pwllheli) and affords nice walks". A fact that will no doubt please the current reader, but is hardly a glowing tribute. The 1923 version of the same guide has a much expanded entry mentioning, along with the good walking, the golf course, the excellent beaches, the trout fishing and several boarding houses.

Just offshore to the east of Abersoch are the two islands, St. Tudwal's East and West. On the bigger eastern island are the remains of a priory. The establishment of such a settlement on this island was undoubtedly helped by the fact that a natural spring exists providing fresh water. St. Tudwal lived in the 5th century and so was a contemporary of other early saints, but there is no evidence that he established a church on this island. The earliest surviving references date from the 13th century but refer to Tudweiliog (Tudwal's Land). The village of Tudweiliog is of course on the mainland to the north, but the use of his name suggests that Tudwal, or his followers, were well established in this area.

The priory on the island is first mentioned in 1291 and by 1410 was occupied by Augustinians. The last reference to it as a working priory dates from 1511. The last person to make a serious attempt to emulate the early saints was one Fr. Hughes, a priest who used to preach along the coast, but was based on the island. He died in 1887.

The situation at Abersoch is not unlike that at Aberdaron in that you cannot stay by the sea to make further progress east, and a diversion inland must be made. This diversion however allows the route to gain height and therefore provide good views of the coastline.

Leave the centre of Abersoch on the Llanbedrog road and follow it round the back of the harbour. Soon the road to Llangian goes off to the left (SW) and 100 yards past this junction is a wide track also to the left and marked with a footpath sign (sketchmap 6.1).

Walk down the track, passing a few cottages, until the main track swings left to the house of Y Felin. A narrower track goes straight on at this point and soon reaches a gate. Through the gate take great care for in a few yards a turn right up the hill must be taken but the track is not at all obvious. In fact it is signed but in summer the hedgerow plants tend to obscure it. If you reach the house of Melinsoch you have gone about 70 yards too far.

As soon as the turn is made the track improves and leads up to a gate in a hedge. Go through the gate and bear left to contour the hillside above the valley bottom. The way lies parallel to, but not close to the hedge. Generally trend right and as the convex crest is reached a stile shows the way. Over the stile keep in the same direction, passing over a plank bridge with a waymark.

Stay on the same level as the track improves and keep walking up the valley which is now quite pronounced. Pass a telegraph pole to a stile then across a meadow with small lakes below in the valley. A stile is reached over a fence and the valley veers gently to the right. A gate is soon seen in a fence and appears to be the natural continuation of the track but the correct line drops left below the gate to find a stile.

Over the stile keep by the fence on the left with further waymarks. It curves round to the left to arrive at a bend in a farm track. Turn right. The track soon starts to rise and swing to the right. After 200 yards just as the angle starts to ease there is a gate on the left. Go through the gate and stay by the fenceline on the right. Pass by a gate in this fence to reach a gate across the line of the route. Go through this and continue in the same direction as the path improves to arrive at a 'T' junction where there is a large slab of rock with a pond at its base. Turn left.

The track though wide can be wet, but the house at Oerddwr is soon reached (see sketchmap 6.1). Follow the main track as it curves round the house to the right. The way is plain. Keep left up the hill at the next track junction then the lane steepens to arrive at a tarmac road at the house called Penrhiwau. Turn right along the road.

Walk along the road for 500 yards or so. There are excellent views of the coast to the right, and the road, being a cul-de-sac, is not much used by traffic. Pass by a couple of small caravan sites until the road swings left and climbs a little. Just after a gate on the right a track leads off to the right just below the house of Tyn yr Ardd. The junction is waymarked.

Follow the track which soon makes an abrupt turn to the right, passes the cottage of Bryn Melyn and drops to a stile. Go over the stile into a hillside meadow with clumps of gorse, but keep in the same line as height is lost. Soon a further stile is reached. Over the stile keep straight on to a bridge. Over the bridge turn left, ignoring the gate in front, and follow the obvious track through the gorse to a gate, steps and another small bridge.

Over the bridge bear right still losing height and stay near the dropping hedgeline. Pass the remains of what appears to be an old stone stile. At this point the better track keeps left but the correct way is down the fainter track keeping parallel to the hedgeline. A mistake is unlikely here for the road can be seen below. Drop to the road to find a small gate giving access to it, just near a bus stop. Turn left.

This is the main road to Llanbedrog, which is only about a mile away. However, the extra time it takes to walk around the headland at Llanbedrog is well worth the effort and unless you are in a particular hurry the next 2 miles should not be missed.

Walk along the main road for 100 yards when a lane goes off to the right (OS Ref: 322311). Take this. Walk for 150 yards and the lane turns right. Stay with it as it steepens and swings left then right to a 'T' junction.

Map watchers will no doubt have noted that use has not been made of a right of way that looks inviting. A brand new road has been constructed higher up the hill which makes the lines of paths on the OS map difficult to follow. The route described here gives easy access to the headland.

At the 'T' junction turn left and walk uphill for 500 yards, passing a couple of picturesque cottages, until just as the lane starts to flatten an even *smaller lane appears on the right with a footpath sign. If a parking area on the left is reached you have gone 50 yards too far.*

Turn up the smaller lane past further cottages, keeping right at a junction after which the lane degenerates into a stony track. Keep on this track ignoring a couple of tracks off to the right and soon the open top of the headland is reached. There are good views all around.

It is impossible to describe the tracks around the headland for there are so many variations, but they are all easy to follow. The best advice is to stay as near as is reasonably practicable to the cliff tops. There is a lot of gorse about and it overhangs some of the tracks - definitely not a place for shorts!

The apex of the headland is soon reached with good views of the beaches to the west and the east. Much of the South Lleyn Coast follows the same pattern as can be seen here, with occasional head-lands separating long stretches of sand or pebbles. The hea-lands represent the bands of harder rock which have been resistant to the erosive power of the sea. This headland is composed of a hard granite por-phery.

From the tip of the headland the way now turns north-west to approach the village of

The Iron Man sculpture set high on the headland at Llanbedrog

Llanbedrog. The tracks hereabouts tend to converge on a statue called the Iron Man for reasons that won't leave you guessing. It is marked as a 'statue' on the OS map. From the Iron Man a track leads steeply down the cliffside and the way is well trodden. It is very steep and despite the handrails you will need to take extra care. The track soon emerges at the beach.

Turn left past an elegant stone boathouse and across the beach. Go past the house called Foxhole with its fuscia bushes to where a road comes in by the side of some tea-rooms. The road is the main access to the beach from the village, and a gentle walk up its leafy valley soon brings you out at a road junction by St. Pedrog's church.

Very little seems to be known about St. Pedrog, except that he had Cornish connections and established his church hereabouts some time in the 6th century. This makes him a contemporary of several of the other saints of the Lleyn, but there is no evidence that Pedrog had connections with Bardsey.

Just below St. Pedrog's church is the imposing house of Plas Glyn-y-Weddw. This was built in the Gothic style in the 1850s and sold in 1896 to a businessman from Cardiff who opened the house up as an art gallery and tea-rooms. The venture achieved some popularity, but during the second world war the house was requisitioned for use by land army girls. After the war it was neglected until 1979 when it again changed hands and reverted to its earlier role as an art gallery. Musical and other cultural events are also held at the house.

Walk up the road, passing St. Pedrog's on the left, to a junction (sketchmap 6.2 p122). Bear left and walk up the road, passing St. Pedrog's church hall, and continue up the steepening hill. Soon the road curves to the left to expose a large pub, Glan y Weddw. The pub stands at a road junction with a sign to Aberdaron, Myntho, Botwnnog and Sarn Melteryn. On the opposite side of the road from the pub is a footpath leading through a churchyard (see photograph p123). Walk along the footpath to emerge behind some garages, then walk round them into a quiet suburban road. Carry on up the road to a junction and turn right.

Walk past the derestriction signs (you can speed up if you wish) and very soon a footpath sign points the way down a track on the left, just before the house of Glascoed Golygfa. The track swings right then left and then a waymark can be seen on the right with two gates side by side (see

Leaving Llanbedrog
Sketchmap 6.2

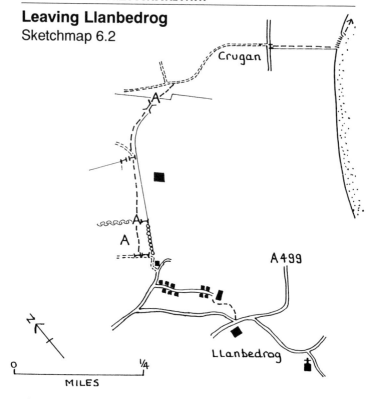

photograph). *Go through the gates and alongside the wall, passing a lonely stile which has no purpose. Continue in the same line through another gate and down to a stone stile. Keep walking alongside the very high stone wall through a further gate and then drop straight down to a stream. (A good track goes off to the left but should be ignored.)*

The stream is crossed by a bridge to an adjacent stile. Over the stile bear right and follow a narrow track up the hillside until it joins a wide farm track. Turn right. Stay on this farm track over the cattle grid and past Crugan Farm to emerge on the main road (OS Ref: 335224). Go straight across the road to a gate leading into a field (see photograph p124). The path across the field is not a right of way but access is allowed by the landowner.

Leaving Llanbedrog.
The picture was taken from the front of the pub called Glan y Weddw

The tracks to the north of Llanbedrog walking towards Crugan Farm

The exit from Crugan Farm as the route crosses the main Llanbedrog to Pwllheli road

Llanbedrog →

The eastern end of the beach at Llanbedrog and the headland of Carreg y Defaid

*The small bay east of Carreg y Defaid and the gate on the
unmade lane which leads to Pwllheli*

*Stay by the hedgeline to the top of the cliffs where a gate leads onto a narrow
track with steps and a handrail down to the beach (see photograph).*

*Turn left along the beach and make for the headland of Carreg y Defaid
some 500 yards away (OS Ref: 343325). Clamber round the rocks of the
headland to drop into a small bay. If you are lucky you may find pebbles of
purple amethyst but not of a quality to be valuable. Look across the bay to
see a large boulder breakwater. A gate is visible on the far side of the bay
above the breakwater (see photograph). Aim for the gate and walk round the
back of the bay, alongside the breakwater, for about 100 yards. At some
suitable point clamber over the boulders and bear right across the grass to
reach the gate and a wide track. Turn right onto the track.*

*Keep straight on along the track, through a series of gates, but avoiding
occasional side tracks to the right. These in any case only lead onto the
beach. The track stays parallel to the shore. Pass a modern bungalow and
the ruin of Tyddyncaled until a further gate leads into a green lane. Keep
straight on as a golf course appears on the left, and just after the clubhouse
the track swings to the left to emerge onto the edge of a housing estate. Do
not go up the road to the right, but go straight across the mouth of the golf
club entrance to a gate and footpath sign leading onto a leafy footpath*

behind some houses.

The path is very plain and soon reaches a further gate. The way curves to the right and over a narrow bridge. At this point the track splits. Take the left-hand branch to a bigger bridge over a small river and thence to the main road. Turn right and walk into Pwllheli.

CYCLISTS

There are no suitable cycle tracks on leaving Abersoch and the road to Llanbedrog must be followed for a while. From the centre of Abersoch, drop down to the harbour and then onto the main A499 road that climbs out of the town to the north-east. The holiday development known as the Warren soon appears on the right. About 2 miles out of Abersoch a lane forks off to the left (OS Ref: 318302). The junction is marked by a sign that states "The Warren Touring Park - Touring Caravans and tents - Families only" (sketchmap 6.1).

Turn left down the lane but just before the entrance to the caravan site, note a gate on the left which states "Ty'n Coed - Private Road". The road might well be private but there is a bridleway running along it so pass through the gate and cycle up the lane to the farm. Pass through the farmyard between the house and the barn and climb the slight rise towards a gate. As height is gained it becomes clear that there are two gates, the right-hand one being further back (see photograph). Go through the right-hand gate and drop down a track for 30 yards to the top of a field. Turn left along the hedgeline through a fine crop of thistles (see photograph). Follow the hedgeline, which is actually the boundary of an old and totally overgrown green lane, to the corner of the field. Turn right along the hedgeline to drop down the field to a stream.

Cross the stream and ride up the opposite bank bearing slightly left on an improving track which leads in 300 yards to a gate. Turn right up the unmade lane and continue up the hill to a tarmac lane. Turn right along the lane. Stay on the lane as it takes a sharp turn to the left after 400 yards and then climbs gently to a 'T' junction with the main B4413 road. Turn right and follow this road for the mile or so into Llanbedrog.

The headland walk, described below at (a), is excellent but not legally available to bikers. To sample the delights of this area it is

The route through the farm of Tyn-y-coed. The correct line goes into the trees as indicated to reach a gate

Part of the cycling route between Abersoch and Llanbedrog just after the farm of Tyn-y-coed

necessary to padlock the bikes for a while, and take an interlude on foot.

Leave Llanbedrog to the north-east on the A499 road signposted to Pwllheli. Just under a mile along the main road is a minor road bearing off to the right, which is shown as a cul-de-sac. On the main road the place is marked by a side road sign and is soon after the cottage called Bwthyr Crug. Turn down the cul-de-sac and a narrow ramp at its end to reach a little bay. At the back of the bay is a large breakwater made from boulders and in the distance is a gate on top of the boulder line (see photograph p125). For the second time on this circuit there is a section where the bikes must be carried. Go round the back of the bay and along the base of the boulders for about 100 yards then scramble up the boulders to the field at the top. Bear right to reach the gate and a wide track. Pass through the gate and cycle east along the track.

Cycle along the track, ignoring other tracks bearing off to the right, until a golf clubhouse is passed on the left. The track now swings left to join a suburban road by the entrance to the golf club. Turn right along the road past the rows of neat bungalows and thence into the centre of Pwllheli.

OTHER WALKS IN THIS AREA

a) Llanbedrog Headland

Start:	Llanbedrog by St Pedrog's church
Car park:	Car park towards the beach. Village well served by buses
OS Ref:	329316
Distance:	2^{1}/$_{2}$ miles
Ascent:	350ft
Grade:	B (very steep descent despite the handrails)

Much of this walk is covered on the main route, but it is such a delightful headland that it is worth describing the links that can make this into a circular walk.

Start from the prominent St. Pedrog's church in Llanbedrog. Walk up the road, away from the beach, bearing left at the junction. Walk up the road for a short distance and then turn left in front of

Criccieth castle from the west
Ynys Cyngar, east of Black Rock

Approaching Portmadoc harbour
Borth-y-Gest

St. Pedrog's church hall into Craig y Llan. Stay on this lane, climbing quite steeply. It soon curves to the right, and you should ignore the footpath sign at this point. The lane continues to climb and in 400 yards there are two more footpath signs, but you should resist the temptation for a while yet.

Eventually the lane stops climbing and levels out. There is a car parking spot on the right and a little lane turns off to the left, also with a footpath sign. This is the main way onto the headland. Turn left and walk up, passing the cottages and bearing right at the lane junction. The tarmac disappears at this point and the track leads up onto the open headland. This is now part of the main route and is fully described above. This will bring you back in due course to St. Pedrog's church.

b) Abersoch circular

Start:	Abersoch, behind the harbour
Car park:	No problems, also good bus service
OS Ref:	313283
Distance:	4 miles
Ascent:	225ft
Grade:	C

A pleasant walk into the low hills behind Abersoch. Whilst the walk is not exciting it does give good views of the coast, and is short enough to use as an evening stroll.

The first part of the walk follows the main route as it leaves Abersoch from near the harbour. It enters the small and neglected valley behind Abersoch as described in the early paragraphs of this chapter. When the part of the route that is described thus .."After 200 yards just as the angle starts to ease there is a gate on the left" is reached this walk parts company with the main route. The main route goes off through the gate but this walk continues up the wide track through a gate. Stay with this track, passing through more gates and by a farm at Muriau (OS Ref: 311301). The track crests a slight rise and begins to gently descend towards the sea.

At this point there is a track junction and the way lies sharp right, up the hill to a gate by a ruin. Pass through the gate and strike out across the field bearing slightly left. You are heading for a stile on the other side of the field, but as the land is convex at this point it is necessary to walk part way across the field to see it. Pass over the stile and still bearing left drop to a gate just by a garage which serves a big house on the left (E).

Walk alongside the garage to emerge at a 'T' shaped lane junction. On the right-hand side of the junction made by the 'T' is a footpath heading south-east (OS Ref: 312293). Take this to keep your height as the path contours on a small escarpment above a grassy bowl which is full of caravans. There are excellent views over the coast, if not in the foreground. Pass through a gate as the track improves and soon gets a tarmac covering. Continue along the road to meet the main Abersoch road where a right turn soon leads back to the harbour.

CHAPTER 7
Pwllheli to Portmadoc

Pwllheli lays claim to be the 'capital' of the Lleyn, being the largest town and a major shopping and market centre. It is also the terminus of the railway from Portmadoc. It is certainly a bustling and busy place. The town has a long history having been given its charter by the Black Prince in 1355. It was well known as a fishing port in the 16th century. It also developed a shipbuilding trade that only declined in the late 19th century when Portmadoc took over the mantle of the major port of the area. Even then Pwllheli held some importance and in 1903 the harbour was dredged and enlarged at a cost of £70,000, so somebody must have thought the town had potential.

These days the harbour is used mainly for pleasure craft, but Pwllheli does not spring to mind when one is thinking of seaside resorts on the Lleyn. There is the Butlins holiday camp to the east of the town, but it is rare to hear of anyone going to Pwllheli for their holidays. This was not always the case and only 60 years ago Pwllheli was a highly regarded resort. One guidebook of the 1920s describes the beach as "one of the finest in the kingdom" and sums up the town thus: "Pwllheli is a health resort abounding in beauty and loveliness, and rich in health giving properties".

In terms of clues to the Bardsey pilgrims Pwllheli is seriously lacking. No evidence of early saints is found here. They obviously did not appreciate its "health giving properties". The parish church dates from 1887, despite being built in an earlier style, and is dedicated to St. Peter.

Walk through the town of Pwllheli, staying on the Portmadoc road until the railway station is reached. This is opposite the tourist office. Walk past the front of the station and a small cafe and take the next road left. Continue along this road, with the harbour on the right, to a crossroads. Turn right. In 100 yards another road goes off to the left signed "Glan y Don" industrial estate. Walk down the road through the small industrial estate until the road bends to the right and a track goes straight ahead. At

*Leaving Pwllheli. The route lies round the back of the harbour,
and then through the unattractive industrial estate to reach this point
where a footpath leads out onto the beach*

this point is a sign to a woodyard called Coed Stockwood (see photograph)

Continue along the track past the woodyard. The track curves round
to the right, towards the sea, and some wooden steps soon take you over the
dunes to reach the shore. Turn left (north-east) and walk along the shore
for about a mile. The turn-off from the beach is a little difficult because the
line of dunes obscures any landmarks. Points to watch for are the wooden
steps leading up the dunes, and shortly after these there is a gap in the fence
and a gap between the dunes (OS Ref: 403359). This leads onto a narrow
lane leading to a caravan site and a small Halt on the railway line.

The route however leaves the lane as soon as you have passed through
the dunes and takes a track on the right leading east. Go through the gate
(take your pick, there are two side by side) and walk along the track which
stays parallel to the line of dunes. After 1/2 mile the wide track curves left
to a gate. Ignore the gate and keep straight on a narrower track. This soon
becomes indistinct and one must cross over the dunes onto the beach.

Walk along the beach for some 200 yards where there is a sandy bluff,
a dune that is somewhat higher than the rest. At this point you must bear
left (ENE). According to the OS map there is a right of way across the land
behind the dunes. Be warned - it is not easy to find and there is no track to

speak of. In fact there are a number of narrow trods, some of which are better than others. The correct right of way passes Ty'n-y-morfa (OS Ref: 417358) and Pant-yr-aur (OS Ref: 422358). Despite the lack of an obvious path the routefinding is very easy for you just need to aim at the large pylon in the distance. This pylon is in fact the support for an aerial ropeway at the Butlins holiday camp which is now quite close.

Whichever of the various narrow tracks you have followed across the sandy country behind the dunes, as long as you aim at the pylon, a good wide track will be reached at some point. If you are doing this section in a thick sea mist then a compass bearing will be necessary. Turn left on the wide track. Follow this track in a generally northerly direction, ignoring other tracks coming in from the left. Soon a gate appears above a cottage. Keep on in the same direction and the track develops into a lane which passes a small railway station serving Butlin's camp. At the top of the lane is a 'T' junction and the main Pwllheli to Portmadoc road. Turn right and pass the camp's main entrance.

The main road is very busy at this point so take care. In 200 yards or so a wide track appears on the left (leading NNE). There is a chapel on the corner (OS Ref: 432370). The track is shown as a "white" road on the map, and is, for the most part, a pleasant green lane. Turn along the track and soon swing right with it to approach a modern house. The track swings left in front of the house to a gate. Pass through the gate and stay on the obvious track for just over ¹/₂ mile until a lane is reached on the outskirts of the village of Chwilog (OS Ref: 429383). Turn right.

Follow the lane as it curves to the left to join the main road through the village of Chwilog. The village appears a sleepy little place but there are shops, a pub and a post office. The village does not have any particular significance relating to the Pilgrims Route to Bardsey, but you are driven inland at this point in order to get around the Butlins camp.

Turn right along the main road and walk through the village. At the main road junction bear left, staying on the major road, and continue for ¹/₂ mile. The road drops into a valley and then climbs out on the other side. Just as the road begins to level out at the top of the hill there is a post box on the left and a green lane crosses the main road. This is Lon Goed, a superb tree lined avenue cutting across the countryside, giving pleasant and easy walking. Turn left and head north-west.

After a mile a small settlement with a chapel is seen on the left and in another ¹/₂ mile you must turn off the Lon Goed to start moving back towards the coast. The Lon Goed swings gently left at the point where a sign shows "Ty Croes". There is a wide track on the right, much the same standard as the Lon Goed but without the obvious trees lining the sides (OS Ref: 456393). Turn along this track for 150 yards to reach a lane where there is a sign for "Ty Croes" and "Hidiart Lyndan". Turn right.

Walk along the lane to pass a lodge. There is a turn to the right here which is ignored. Continue along the lane as it drops steeply down into some woods and then a road junction. Turn left here across the bridge which spans the Afon Dwyfach. Eventually a 'T' junction is met. Turn right and then walk along the road until a junction with a wider road is reached. Turn left and gently lose height as you approach the village of Llanystumdwy. Keep on the road passing the church and cross the bridge over the Afon Dwyfor in the centre of the village.

The village of Llanystumdwy is famous as the home of David Lloyd George, that most famous of Welsh politicians and Prime Minister from 1916 to 1922. In fact Lloyd George was born in Manchester in 1863 but his father died when David was just 18 months old and his mother took him back to the family home in Llanystumdwy. At the age of sixteen he joined a firm of solicitors in Portmadoc and in 1884 set up his own practice in Criccieth.

Lloyd George had always taken an interest in politics and in 1890 the sudden death of the MP for Caernarfon led to a by-election. Lloyd George won the seat by just 18 votes but he held on to it for the next 55 years. The village is full of sites relevant to Lloyd George and his family and is well worth exploring. There is a circular walk at the end of this chapter that visits the village and the site of Lloyd George's grave.

Returning to the main route, just a few yards from the bridge are the lawns of the Dwyfor Cafe on the right, and a footpath sign showing the route heading south past the Dwyfor Cafe. Take this footpath (sketchmap 7.1), past the back of some houses, to emerge on the main Portmadoc road. Go straight across the road to a farm lane. Both sides of the road have footpath signs. Pass through the gate still heading south towards the sea and follow the farm lane to reach the farmhouse of Aberkin (OS Ref: 471381).

The rights of way as shown on the OS map have been changed in this area, so take care. In fact the new right of way is easier to follow than the old so the next reprint of the map should make life easier, but until then follow the directions herewith carefully. Sketchmap 7.1 shows the new situation.

The farm lane soon passes barns on the left and then it turns to the left at the farmhouse itself. The track soon comes to a gate but there are some concrete steps on the right. Climb over and pick up the track for just a few yards when it turns to the right. Ignore this turn for straight ahead is a gate with a stile. Go over the stile and follow the fenceline on your right. Drop into some trees as the track veers slightly right to a further gate and stile. Go over the stile and keep straight on to cross

Llanystumdwy to Criccieth
Sketchmap 7.1

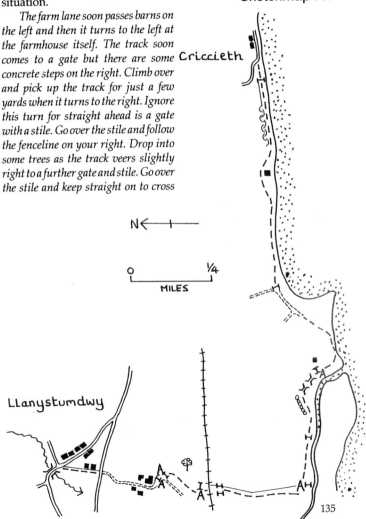

135

the railway line and then to a further gate. Go through this gate, and ignoring gates to left and right, follow the line of the fence on the left. It bears slightly left then straightens out. Walk down the meadow until stopped by the waters of the Afon Dwyfor, then turn left over the stile. The route is now back with the OS right of way at Ref: 473373.

The next section needs little description for you follow the bank of the river until it reaches the sea. All the stiles are in place and someone has even provided little log bridges over the muddier parts. Shortly after passing a shed to your left the shoreline appears. Turn left (E) and walk for just a few yards over the beach then keep to the back of the beach, away from the sea, to pick up a track travelling east behind the bay. Soon a wider track comes in from the left, so the way improves, still keeping at the back of the beach. The better track soon swings away again to the left, but at this point a gate is directly in front and the original narrow track goes by it.

The narrow track now winds its way to the top of a line of cliffs. However the rock hereabouts is sand, gravel and boulder clay and is very soft. The effects of the sea crashing into such soft strata are easy to see in the landslips and collapses, which in places have caused the path to divert. Climb up to the house of Cefn Castell, which itself appears in some danger from erosion, but still keeping parallel to the seashore below. The track improves after Cefn Castell, and after passing between some high hedges arrives at a gate leading onto the promenade at Criccieth. The famous castle is now directly in front and it is good to reach it at last, as it has been in sight for some miles.

Criccieth has been a seaside resort since Victorian times, the fine setting of the castle making it an imposing site. Unlike many of the castles in North Wales this was not established by Edward I although he did expand and improve the previous version. The inner part of the castle was built by Llywelyn the Great some time before 1240 AD. Llywelyn was one of the most famous of the Welsh princes and largely succeeded in unifying the warring Welsh factions of the time. The castle was improved with extra outer defences by Llywelyn the Last before his death in battle in 1282.

The castle was improved further by Edward I and Edward II and became part of the ring of defences that enabled the English kings of the time to keep the Welsh subdued. The castle was captured again by the Welsh under the leadership of Owain Glyndwr and it was so thoroughly destroyed that scorch marks from the flames can

The eastern bay at Criccieth with the castle prominent on the headland

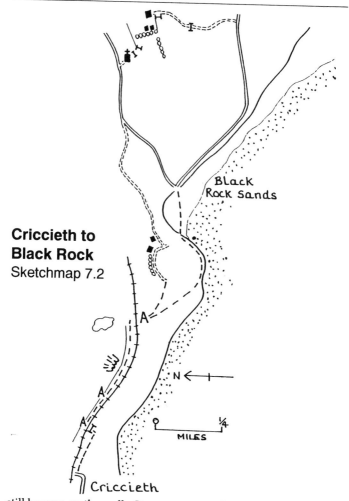

**Criccieth to
Black Rock**
Sketchmap 7.2

Black
Rock Sands

still be seen on the walls. It was never used again.

As a seaside resort Criccieth seems to have had a slow start. A guidebook of 1878 notes that "There are comfortable lodgings enough.... but they are not numerous" and further on states ".. we

138

Leaving Criccieth. At the end of the eastern promenade this road leads up towards the railway track. Just prior to the railway a gate on the right gives access to a narrow path

would just hint to Welsh builders that the more English the comforts they introduce into their dwellings the better they will be patronised". The local builders must have taken note of this because in a guidebook of 1919 the following is written: "Criccieth... is generally regarded as being the most natural of all the Welsh watering places... for the most part its buildings are modern villas ...". The town retains its air of genteel tranquillity and thankfully has not been overtaken by amusement arcades and fast food outlets.

Walk along the promenade towards the castle, with the row of Victorian hotels and guesthouses on the left. The road swings to the left under the castle and then climbs the hill. Stay hard by the castle grounds until on cresting the rise the next bay is seen. Drop down the road and onto the promenade which is followed to its end (OS Ref: 505382). Turn left here (NE) and walk the few yards to the railway line (sketchmap 7.2 and photograph). Do not cross the line but turn right parallel to the railway on an obvious footpath. For the next mile the path follows the line of the railway. After about 300 yards a stile leads to a crossing and the path then

The approach to Black Rock - the route around the headland involves a rocky scramble down to the sands. For those of more pedestrian tastes a route to the left should be taken as shown

continues on the other side of the railway. The path soon passes through a cutting and at this point is very close to the rails so take extra care.

Soon the railway starts to swing inland but a stile on the right gives access to meadows leading back to the shore (OS Ref: 519377). Carefully cross the rails and go over the stile. At this point there is a choice of routes depending on your propensity for rock scrambling. Ahead, to the south-east, is the rocky headland of Craig Ddu. It can be navigated either to the left (inland side) or right (sea side). The right-hand route is more scenic but has a sting in the tail - the photograph shows the two options.

For those who enjoy having to use their hands as well as feet to make progress the route lies across the meadow aiming for the point where Craig Ddu drops into the sea. The rocks are soon reached and the headland should be followed round to the left until a narrow track leads to the top of a gully through the cliffline. The sands of Black Rock are 30ft below. Descend the gully, with the hardest moves just above the sands, to reach the beach. Walk to the back of the beach to pick up the lane running inland alongside the caravan site (OS Ref: 527375). Walk up the lane to a point where it veers right and a farm track comes in from the left. Those who elected not to take the scrambling route re-join the main route at this point (OS Ref: 529378).

Those readers who wish to avoid the pleasures of scrambling down the rocks should cross the meadows aiming at the high point of Craig Ddu. As the flats of the meadow rise up to the hillside turn left (NE) and walk along a wide stony cart track which swings to the right as it gains height. Soon a stone cottage is seen on the left below. Keep bearing right at this point and climb to the high point of the track where views of Black Rock sands open up. At the drystone wall turn left and pass the buildings at Pentrip (OS Ref: 525377) to drop onto a farm road heading north-east. Follow this to the lane where the two routes come together again (see previous paragraph).

Continue along the lane away from the sea, and steeply up the hill for 400 yards until the small church of St. Michael's is seen on the right (OS Ref: 534378). Walk into the church grounds and round to its south side. Cross the small graveyard to its south-east corner where a gate gives access to a track running down the hillside. This is a magnificent viewpoint. Drop down the track and through another gate, then turn left to a stone wall, then right to pass the barns. Turn left after passing the end of the barns just after a gap in a stone wall. Cross to a gate below the house at Glan-y-morfa-mawr (OS Ref: 536377). Go through the gate and turn right down the unmade road which swings right then left to another gate. At this point it is possible to bear left down the hillside on a track. This is not marked on the map as a right of way but seems well used. To be certain of staying legal use the farm road. In either case a road soon appears.

On reaching the road turn left (E) and walk along it for 200 yards until houses appear. Soon a footpath sign indicates a right turn into a large caravan site at Garreg Goch. The right of way through the site is marked by signs but take care because there are also many site roads and paths. Walk into the site until faced by a shop. Turn left in front of the shop then right by the side of a garage. The track narrows and bears left to come out

141

Black Rock to Borth-y-Gest

Sketchmap 7.3

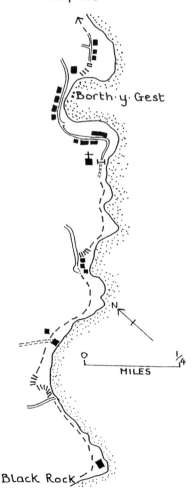

on a wider camp road. Bear left to a road junction and here turn right. At the next junction turn right along the public road passing the Glanaber Pub on the way to the beach (OS Ref: 544366). The campsite is a confusing place, but don't worry if you lose direction as the main objective is to arrive on the beach at some point!

On reaching the beach turn left (E) along it and head for the rocky outcrop of Ynys Cyngar dead ahead (OS Ref: 554365). Climb the low headland to reach a path that is very well made with wooden slats and steps and which curves round to the left (N) following the coastline (sketchmap 7.3). There is a golf course to the left of the track. This very obvious track is not marked on the OS map but is of recent construction and well used. The back of a bay is soon reached where a lane comes in from the left. Go straight across the lane into the bushes where the track climbs steeply onto the cliff tops. The track soon levels out and continues in an easterly direction following the cliff tops. This is an excellent section with super views over the estuary and the Rhinog hills beyond. The path is so plain that further description is *unnecessary. After a mile of this delightful cliff top the path widens, passes a church on the left and comes onto a road. This is the start of the sleepy little resort of Borth-y-Gest (OS Ref: 565374).*

In the guidebook of 1878, the village was known simply as 'Borth' but no doubt this caused confusion with the larger 'Borth' near Aberystwyth. In 1878 the village was described as "..the neatest and cleanest in Wales". By 1919 it had its full name and was still well regarded as ".. a pretty village ..which offers excellent facilities".

Walk down the road as it bends to the left passing rows of stone cottages. Soon some steps lead off on the right to give access to a car park (with toilets) and what passes for a promenade. Walk along the pavement around the back of the muddy bay, until the point where the main road turns away from the sea. Here bear slightly right (footpath sign) and climb the tarmac footpath up the hill. Keep straight on past several large houses where the path loses the tarmac and narrows. Keep on this path which drops gradually down through the trees to drop onto a road. Turn left and walk along the road. This is the start of the town of Portmadoc and the popularity of sailing can be seen by the various boatyards along the roadside. The road soon reaches a park where a right turn leads to Portmadoc High Street and journey's end. Your pilgrimage is over.

Portmadoc is a busy shopping centre and tourist resort. It is also very popular with boaters who can take advantage of its fine harbour facilities. The town developed in the 19th century with a trade based on the export of slate. It also developed as a shipbuilding town and had a fine reputation for quality sailing boats that perhaps explains the large number of boatyards and repair shops that were seen on the approach to the town. The town is closely associated with one William Madocks MP who was the driving force behind the large land reclamation project associated with Portmadoc. The story of the project is fascinating but too long to be told here. The local bookshops have a number of publications concerning the town and its growth.

Portmadoc does not provide any information on the saints of Bardsey, or have any connection with the Pilgrims Route. In fact the line of the Pilgrims Route is a little north of Portmadoc but can be visited by reference to walk (c), the Tyn Llan circular, at the end of this chapter.

CYCLISTS

Leave Pwllheli on the north-east side on the A499 signposted to Caernarfon. Follow this road as it climbs up the valley past the BP petrol station. Ignore all side roads until about a mile and a half outside Pwllheli the road levels out, and a small lane appears on the right signposted to Abererch (OS Ref: 385364). Turn down the lane and follow it to a 'T' junction. Turn left and cycle into Abererch village centre.

Stay on the main road through the village, heading generally east until the main Pwllheli to Portmadoc road (A497) is reached. Take care as this is a busy road but you will not be on it for long. Continue south-east on the main road for about 400 yards when a turn-off to the left onto a lane appears (OS Ref: 405365). The junction is marked by the house named Gorwel. The house is not visible but the nameplate is plain to see in the wall. Bear left onto the unmade lane that gives good cycling. The lane gradually gains height then levels off with excellent views on the right towards the coast. The lane then gently descends until it again links with the main road. Take care once again but only for some 500 yards when a left turn is made into a lane, signposted to the medieval house (OS Ref: 421367). Cycle along the lane to reach the old house of Penarth Fawr on the right (OS Ref: 420377).

Penarth Fawr is a rare example of a 'Hall-house' and was constructed in the 15th century. This is the only surviving example in this area of the Lleyn. The house is pleasant from the outside but not exciting. It is more notable for its interior, when the 15th century influence is seen. During the summer months it is open every day from 9.30am to 6.30pm.

After visiting the house continue on the lane as it turns to the right (E) and then veers to the north-east. Ignore a turn-off to the left and stay on the lane until a point where it turns sharply to the left and a minor road goes right (in effect straight on). Take the minor road which has some abrupt corners but leads eventually to the village of Chwilog and a 'T' junction (OS Ref: 432386). Turn right. In 500 yards the road splits and you need to bear left on the B4354 signed to Criccieth. The road drops into a valley and then climbs out on the other side. Just as the road begins to level out at the top of the hill there is a post box on the left (not visible until the last minute) and a tree lined green lane crosses the main road. This is Lon Goed, a superb avenue cutting across the countryside, giving pleasant and easy off road cycling. Note that this lane is popular with walkers and although shown as a white road on the map consideration needs to be given to other users. Turn left and head north-west.

After a mile you pass a small settlement with a chapel on the left and in another $^1/_2$ mile you must turn off the Lon Goed to start moving back towards the coast. The Lon Goed swings gently left at the point where a sign shows "Ty Croes". There is a wide track on the right, much the same standard as the Lon Goed but without the obvious trees lining the sides (OS Ref: 456393). Turn along this track for 150 yards to reach a lane where there is a sign for "Ty Croes" and "Hidiart Lyndan". Turn right.

Cycle along the lane to pass a lodge. There is a turn to the right here which is ignored. Continue along the lane as it drops steeply down into some woods and then a road junction. Turn left here across the bridge which spans the Afon Dwyfach. Eventually a 'T' junction is met. Turn right and then ride along the road until a junction with a wider road is reached. Turn left and gently lose height as you approach the village of Llanystumdwy. Keep on the road passing the church and cross the bridge over the Afon Dwyfor in the centre of the village.

As soon as the river has been crossed a left turn is made, up a lane heading north-east. Those who wish to see more of the village and its associations with Lloyd George should continue into the main part of the village and return to this point in due course. Puff away up the hill, passing the Lloyd George memorial on the left (worth a visit), until the lane levels out. Ignore a turning to the right and in a mile pass a row of terraced cottages to arrive at a 'T' junction with the main road.

For those who need an overnight stop, shops or refreshments a right turn leads downhill into the centre of Criccieth. Those hardy souls who wish to battle on without sampling the delights of the town should turn left. Climb the hill for a mile to a road junction at Gell Farm. Turn right onto a tiny lane, and keep bearing right at the next junction in 400 yards.

Those who decided to visit the flesh pots of Criccieth must climb back up to this lane. However, there is an alternative, if somewhat steep route from the town centre, which provides a little off road interest. At the main crossroads in the town turn left (E) and then almost immediately left again in front of Barclays Bank, up a narrow road with signs to the golf club. Stay on this lane climbing steadily until the golf club is reached on the left.

The lane degenerates into an unmade track and swings right and then left to reach some derelict buildings and large boulders. This point is in the middle of the golf course, and not all members will realise that there is a right of way for cyclists hereabouts, so be prepared to show some tact! From the derelict buildings carry on up the hill bearing slightly left to reach the 5th tee with its bench. Continue in the same line following a line of boulders to reach another tee just by the 13th green. There is a gate to the left which provides an exit from the golf course. Pass through the gate and follow the wide track that veers to the right to join the tiny lane, back on the main route. Turn right.

Stay on this high lane, with magnificent views of the coast, for nearly 2 miles to a 'T' junction (OS Ref: 523402). Turn right and drop down to the main road at Pentrefelin. Cycle for 400 yards to a point where the main road swings gently right and a side road bears left. There is a war memorial at the junction between the two roads and a phone box to the left. Take the left-hand minor road.

The section from Pwllheli has not provided bikers with much excitement off road, but the next couple of miles will help to compensate. Follow the lane as its tarmac soon disappears and it climbs and winds its way through the low hills hereabouts. The section is delightful, but is alas all too soon over. However there is some interest near its end.

At the point where the track changes from unmade to tarmac again is a small church on the left. The church is dedicated to St. Bueno, the most famous of all the saints having connections with the Pilgrims Route to Bardsey. Just past the church is a tea-room and country crafts centre. The owners of the tea-room have produced a leaflet which states that the unmade lane which has just been cycled is part of the old Pilgrims Route to Bardsey. This is a statement high on assertion and low on evidence, apart from the church of St. Bueno. Nevertheless it is pleasant to end (for Portmadoc is now just a couple of miles away) the route on a high point.

To complete the ride, continue along the narrow lane past the tea-rooms to arrive at the village of Penmorfa. Turn right onto the main A487 road and cycle towards Tremadoc. At the road junction with the A498 bear left, still towards Tremadoc. 200 yards past the junction is a footpath sign on the right and just a few yards past this is an opening on the right, a sort of paved way. Take this paved track (traffic free) which arrives in Portmadoc by the railway station. Turn right to pedal into the centre of the town and journey's end. (Cyclists who wish to complete the full round trip back to Caernarfon should turn left on reaching the A487, signposted to Caernarfon. Cycle for 6 miles along this road to the village of Bryncir where a sign shows the way back onto the Lon Eifion cycleway which leads all the way back to the centre of Caernarfon.)

OTHER WALKS IN THIS AREA

a) In the steps of Lloyd George

Start:	Village of Llanystumdwy
Car park:	Ample space in the village. Well served by buses
OS Ref:	475385
Distance:	7 miles
Ascent:	300ft
Grade:	C

There is much to see in the village of Llanystumdwy, which has to do with the life and times of David Lloyd George. There is the museum, the village school and his house, but all are well described in leaflets that are available in the village. This walk passes by Lloyd George's burial place and then continues along a splendid wooded valley alongside the River Dwyfor. It then crosses open moor to descend into Criccieth. The coast is then followed back to Llanystumdwy. If public transport is used from Criccieth the walk is reduced to 4 miles.

The walk starts in the village by the bridge over the river. Take the minor road leading uphill towards Lloyd George's grave which is soon reached on the left. The monument was designed by Sir Clough Williams-Ellis who is perhaps more famous for being the architect of the Italianate village at Portmerion. Walk through the monument and pick up a track leading north by the side of the river. This is the Afon Dwyfor and it is interesting to note that when Lloyd George received his peerage he became Earl Lloyd George of Dwyfor. It seems certain that he would have sauntered along this path.

The navigation is easy for the next mile or so and the walking delightful. The track is well used and passes through several gates. Eventually a stile is reached and shortly after a broken wall. At this point turn right along the wall and left through an arch to emerge onto a lane. Turn left over the cattle grid to a 'T' junction. Turn right (OS Ref: 488400). Walk along this road for about 400 yards to a crossroads with minor lanes, and a sign to Tyddyn Morthwyl campsite.

Turn right in front of the house and follow a wide track for 75 yards and then peel off to the left on a track leading to a gate. Pass through to reach a further gate. Go through this gate then turn sharp right and walk alongside the old wall with the fence on top of it to arrive at another gate. Pass through onto the open, and sometimes boggy land. The track is narrow but reasonable and bears slightly left under the telegraph wires. A substantial track crosses the line of the route and then some flat stones appear to mark the way and provide solid footing in wet weather. Soon a road is reached. Turn right and drop into the centre of Criccieth in ³/₄ mile.

A return can be made to Llanystumdwy by bus (the service is reasonably frequent) but to complete the walk continue through the town to the promenade on the western side of the castle. Walk along the promenade away from the castle and past the end of the terrace of hotels. Go through a gate onto a track and walk along the cliff top passing the house at Cefn Castell. Bear left at the track junction just after the house, staying parallel to the shore. This section is in fact the main route in reverse.

Stay on tracks which keep to the coastline until the mouth of the river is reached. A right turn inland alongside the river must now be made. The track is well marked and soon passes over a stile, then a small plank bridge assists over some marshy ground. Keep by the river passing through a gate with a footpath sign. The next gate has a stile by it. At this point the right of way has changed from that shown on OS maps so take care. The new way is in fact easier. Go over the stile and turn right, and walk up the field alongside the fence. Near the top of the field the fence veers very slightly to the right and there are gates leading into other fields. Keep straight on to pass through a gate and across the railway line. Keep straight on over a stile by a gate onto a track.

The track continues in the same direction but soon curves to the left through trees to reach a stile and gate by a farm road. Over the stile keep straight on towards the farmhouse to a gate and find some stone steps to the left of the gate. Climb over the steps and continue along the lane which turns to the right. Follow the lane until it emerges on the main Portmadoc road. This is a very busy road so take care. Go straight across the road to a footpath sign giving access to a track running behind some houses. This leads back to the centre of Llanystumdwy.

b) Black Rock and Borth-y-Gest

Start:	Criccieth
Car park:	Park in Portmadoc then use public transport
OS Ref:	505382
Distance:	8 miles
Ascent:	Negligible
Grade:	C - but note alternatives at Black Rock

This is an unusual suggestion for a walk. First, it is not a circular, and resorts to public transport, and second, there is no new ground to tread, for this is just a repeat of the main route. However this is such a pretty section that it is worth doing in its own right.

There is a choice of transport from Portmadoc because there is a rail connection as well as a frequent bus service. The railway station is on the north side of Portmadoc on the road out towards Tremadoc. On arrival in Criccieth by whatever means, walk down to the promenade on the eastern side of the castle and thereafter refer to the description in the main text.

c) Tyn Llan circular

Start:	Hamlet of Tyn Llan (2 miles west of Tremadoc)
Car park:	Reasonable, no public transport

OS Ref:	542403
Distance:	Under 2 miles
Ascent:	120ft
Grade:	C

It may seem strange to include such a short walk that is some distance from the coast. This is part of the final stage of the route that the cyclists have followed. It is included here as a walk because of the connections with Bardsey. First, there is a little church, dedicated to St. Bueno, who, as we now know, was one of the most important of the saints connected with the Pilgrims Route. Secondly, the track leading west from the church is, according to the owners of the nearby cafe, the route that the Bardsey pilgrims took on their journey west.

The hamlet of Tyn Llan is not easy to find. Come out of Tremadoc on the Caernarfon road (A487) until, about a mile out of Tremadoc, the road starts to rise through the village of Penmorfa. Turn left in the village down a little lane (OS Ref: 548406). There is often an advertising board put out at the junction. Continue along the little lane until you can go no further. There is a tea-room on the left, with a small craft centre and museum.

The tiny church can be seen past the tea-rooms and small cottages on the opposite side of the road. This is St. Bueno's. Unhappily it always appears to be locked, which is a pity as it seems to have some excellent stained glass. After coming out of the main gate of the church turn right onto a broad track. This is the road that the Bardsey pilgrims walked, in order to reach the coast near Criccieth. Walk along it for ¹/₂ mile until a gate is seen on the left and a cottage can be seen through the trees. Turn left along the footpath past the front of the cottage. Stay on the track until it comes out at a busy road.

Turn left along the road but in literally a few yards turn left again onto a lane. Follow the lane through the woods past the imposing house of Wern after which the track swings slightly right. Soon a track junction is reached and the way lies to the right past the large base of some ugly pylons. Stay on the track which swings up to meet the lane leading to Tyn Llan. Turn left and walk the ¹/₄ mile back to the tea-rooms.

Appendixes

1
MAPS USED TO COVER THE LLEYN PENINSULA

1:50,000 Landranger	- No:	123 - Lleyn Peninsula
1:25,000 Pathfinder	- Nos:	768 - Caernarfon
		785 - Penygroes
		801 - Llanaelhaearn
		821 - Nefyn & Tudweiliog
		843 - Abersoch & Aberdaron
		822 - Pwllheli

1:25,000 Outdoor Leisure No. 18 Snowdonia - Harlech and Bala or the new OS Leisure maps "Lleyn East" and "Lleyn West" (1:25,000)

2
LIST OF VARIOUS FACILITIES ON THE LLEYN PENINSULA

Place	B & B	Hotel	Pub	Camp	Shops
Caernarfon	yes	yes	yes	yes	yes
Llanwnda	yes	no	yes	no	yes
Penygroes	yes	no	yes	no	yes
Clynnog-fawr	yes	yes	yes	1m SW	yes
Trefor	yes	yes	yes	0.5m E	yes
Llithfaen	no	no	yes	no	yes
Pistyll	yes	no	no	yes	yes
Nefyn	yes	yes	yes	1m NE	yes
Morfa Nefyn	yes	yes	yes	no	yes
Porth Dinllaen	no	no	yes	no	no
Edern	yes	no	yes	no	yes
Towyn	no	no	no	yes	no
Tudweiliog	yes	yes	yes	0.5m W	yes
Porthysgaden	no	no	no	yes	no
Tyddyn	no	no	no	yes	no
Porth Colmon	0.5m SE	no	no	yes	m SE
Aberdaron	yes	yes	yes	yes	yes
Rhiw	yes	no	no	0.5m NE	yes
Llanengan	yes	no	yes	1m E	yes
Abersoch	yes	yes	yes	1.5m S	yes
Llanbedrog	yes	yes	yes	0.5m NW	yes
Pwllheli	yes	yes	yes	2m E	yes
Chwilog	yes	no	yes	no	yes
Llanystumdwy	yes	no	yes	yes	yes
Criccieth	yes	yes	yes	2m NE	yes
Black Rock	yes	no	yes	yes	yes
Borth-y-Gest	yes	no	no	no	yes
Portmadoc	yes	yes	yes	0.5m W	yes

3
PUBLIC TRANSPORT

The whole of the Lleyn is covered by bus services. However the existence and frequency of such services can change from year to year. Persons hoping to use public transport are advised to check on the current information. Generally the further west you travel the less frequent and more expensive the service becomes.

Bus timetables are available from tourist information offices, bus and train stations. Alternatively a 9" by 6" self addressed envelope can be sent to:

County Planning Officer
County Offices
Caernarfon
Gwynedd
LL55 1SH

There is also a train service between Portmadoc and Pwllheli, with intermediate stops at Criccieth and 'Starcoast World' (Butlins).

BIBLIOGRAPHY

The Gossiping Guide to Wales - 1878 version
The Gossiping Guide to Wales - 1923 version
The Ward Lock Red Guide to Wales - 1919
Royal Commission on Ancient Monuments - Inventory of
    Caernarvonshire 1960

Burras & Stiff - *Walks on the Lleyn Peninsula*
Chitty, Mary - *The Monks on Ynys Enlli*
Doble, G.H. - *Lives of the Welsh Saints*
Foster & Daniel - *Prehistoric and Early Wales*
Hankin, Elissa R. - *Traditions of the Welsh Saints*
Miller, Molly - *The Saints of Gwynedd*
Nash-Williams - *The Early Christian Monuments in Wales*
Robinson & Millward - *The British Coast*
Senior, Michael - *Harlech & Lleyn, the history of south-west Gwynedd*

NOTES

CICERONE GUIDE BOOKS
LONG DISTANCE WALKS

There are many Cicerone guides to long distance walks in Britain or abroad, which make a memorable holiday or shorter break.

GENERAL TREKKING

THE TREKKER'S HANDBOOK *Thomas R. Gilchrist* Everything a trekker needs to know, from gear to health. *ISBN 1 85284 205 9 A5 size £10.99*

FAR HORIZONS Adventure Travel for All! *Walt Unsworth* From European trails to Himalayan treks; from deserts of Central Asia to jungles of Borneo; from wild-water rafting to gorges of the Yangste. Based on the author's wide experience of this growing form of holiday travel. *ISBN 1 85284 228 8 160pp A5 size £8.99*

LAKE DISTRICT & NORTHERN ENGLAND

THE CUMBRIA WAY AND ALLERDALE RAMBLE *Jim Watson.* A guide to two popular Lake District long distance walks. *ISBN 1 85284 242 3 £6.99*

THE EDEN WAY *Charlie Emett* Through a romantic part of Cumbria. Breaks into sections by using the popular Settle-Carlisle railway. *ISBN 1 85284 040 4 192pp £5.99*

IN SEARCH OF WESTMORLAND *Charlie Emett* A walk around the old county. Full of rich anecdotes and history. *ISBN 0 902363 66 2 200pp £5.50*

WALKING ROUND THE LAKES *John & Anne Nuttall* The ideal walk encompassing all the major summits, yet with high and low level alternatives. *ISBN 1 85284 099 4 240pp £6.99*

WESTMORLAND HERITAGE WALK *Chris Wright and Mark Richards* A circular walk around the old county. *ISBN 0 902363 94 8 256pp PVC cover £7.99*

THE DALES WAY *Terry Marsh* A practical handbook to a very popular walk. With Accommodation Guide. *ISBN 1 85284 102 8 136pp £5.99*

THE DOUGLAS VALLEY WAY *Gladys Sellers* Through the heart of Lancashire. *ISBN 1 85284 073 0 72pp £4.99*

HADRIAN'S WALL Vol 1: The Wall Walk *Mark Richards* Mark conducts you along the wall, accompanied by his skilful maps and sketches. *ISBN 1 85284 128 1 224pp £7.99*

THE ISLE OF MAN COASTAL PATH *Aileen Evans* The Raad ny Foillan path encircles the island; the Herring Way and the Millennium Way are also described. *ISBN 0 902363 95 6 144pp £5.99*

LAUGHS ALONG THE PENNINE WAY *Pete Bogg* Anyone who has struggled through the bogs of the Pennine Way will identify with the humour of this cartoon book. An ideal gift. *ISBN 0 902363 97 2 104pp £2.99*

A NORTHERN COAST TO COAST WALK *Terry Marsh* The most popular LD walk in Britain. Includes accommodation guide. *ISBN 1 85284 126 5 280pp £7.99*

THE RIBBLE WAY *Gladys Sellers* From sea to source close to a junction with the Pennine Way. *ISBN 1 85284 107 9 112pp £5.99*

THE REIVER'S WAY *James Roberts* 150 miles around Northumberland. *ISBN 1 85284 130 3 112pp £5.99*

THE TEESDALE WAY *Martin Collins* A new walk which follows the Tees from its source to the sea. 100 miles, 8 stages. *ISBN 1 85284 198 2 112pp £7.99*

WALKING THE CLEVELAND WAY & THE MISSING LINK *Malcolm Boyes* Circular tour of the North York Moors, including some of our finest coastline. *ISBN 1 85284 014 5 144pp £6.99*

WHITE PEAK WAY *Robert Haslam* An 80-mile walk through the Derbyshire Dales with full details of youth hostels, pubs etc. *ISBN 1 85284 056 0 96pp £4.99*

WEEKEND WALKS IN THE PEAK DISTRICT *John & Anne Nuttall* Magnificent weekend outings illustrated with John's fine drawings. *ISBN 1 85284 137 0 296pp £9.99*

THE VIKING WAY *John Stead* From Barton-upon-Humber to Rutland Water. *ISBN 1 85284 057 9 172pp £5.99*

WALES & THE WELSH BORDER

THE LLEYN PENINSULA COASTAL PATH *John Cantrell.* Starting at Caernarfon the coastal path goes round the peninsula to Porthmadog following the old Bardsey Pilgrims' route. Described for walkers and cyclists, with additional day walks. *ISBN 1 85284 252 0*

WALKING OFFA'S DYKE PATH *David Hunter* Along the Welsh Marches, 170 miles from Chepstow to Prestatyn. *ISBN 1 85284 160 5 224pp £8.99*

THE PEMBROKESHIRE COASTAL PATH *Dennis R. Kelsall* One of Britain's most beautiful paths. includes accommodation guide. *ISBN 1 85284 186 9 200pp £9.99*

SARN HELEN *Arthur Rylance & John Cantrell* The length of Wales in the footsteps of the Roman legions. *ISBN 1 85284 101 X 248pp £8.99*

WALKING DOWN THE WYE *David Hunter* 112 mile walk from Rhayader to Chepstow. *ISBN 1 85284 105 2 192pp £6.99*

A WELSH COAST TO COAST WALK - Snowdonia to Gower *John Gillham* An ideal route for backpackers, away from waymarked trails. *ISBN 1 85284 218 0 152pp £7.99*

SOUTHERN ENGLAND

THE COTSWOLD WAY *Kev Reynolds* A guide to this popular walk. *ISBN 1 85284 049 8 168pp £6.99*

THE GRAND UNION CANAL WALK *Clive Holmes* Along the canal which links the Black Country to London, through rural England *ISBN 1 85284 206 7 128pp £5.99*

THE KENNET & AVON WALK *Ray Quinlan* 90 miles along riverside and canal, from Westminster to Avonmouth, full of history, wildlife, delectable villages and pubs. *ISBN 1 85284 090 0 200pp £6.99*

AN OXBRIDGE WALK *J.A. Lyons* Over 100 miles linking the university cities of Oxford and Cambridge. *ISBN 1 85284 166 4 168pp £7.99*

THE SOUTHERN COAST-TO-COAST WALK *Ray Quinlan* The equivalent of the popular northern walk. 283 miles from Weston-super-Mare to Dover. ISBN 1 85284 117 6 200pp £6.99

THE SOUTH DOWNS WAY & THE DOWNS LINK *Kev Reynolds* A guide to these popular walks. ISBN 1 85284 023 4 136pp £5.99

SOUTH WEST WAY - A Walker's Guide to the Coast Path Vol.1 Minehead to Penzance *Martin Collins* ISBN 1 85284 025 0 184pp PVC cover £8.99
Vol.2 Penzance to Poole *Martin Collins* ISBN 1 85284 026 9 198pp PVC cover £8.99
Two volumes which cover the spectacular coastal path around Britain's south-west peninsula.

THE TWO MOORS WAY *James Roberts* 100 miles crossing Dartmoor, the villages of central Devon and Exmoor to the coast at Lynmouth. ISBN 1 85284 159 1 100pp £5.99

THE WEALDWAY & THE VANGUARD WAY *Kev Reynolds* Two LD walks in Kent, from the outskirts of London to the coast. ISBN 0 902363 85 9 160pp £4.99

SCOTLAND

THE WEST HIGHLAND WAY *Terry Marsh* A practical guide to this very popular walk. ISBN 1 85284 235 0 £6.99

IRELAND

THE IRISH COAST TO COAST WALK *Paddy Dillon* From Dublin and the Wicklows to Valencia Island on the Kerry coast, linking various trails. ISBN 1 85284 211 3 £7.99

FRANCE

THE BRITTANY COASTAL PATH *Alan Castle* The GR34, 360 miles takes a month to walk. Easy access from UK means it can be split into several holidays. ISBN 1 85284 185 0 296pp £10.99

THE CORSICAN HIGH LEVEL ROUTE - Walking the GR20 *Alan Castle* The most challenging of the French LD paths - across the rocky spine of Corsica. ISBN 1 85284 100 1 104pp £5.99

THE PYRENEAN TRAIL: GR10 *Alan Castle* From the Atlantic to the Mediterranean at a lower level than the Pyrenean High Route. 50 days but splits into holiday sections. ISBN 1 85284 245 8 · 176pp £8.99

THE ROBERT LOUIS STEVENSON TRAIL *Alan Castle* 140 mile trail in the footsteps of Stevenson's *'Travels with a Donkey'* through the Cevennes. ISBN 1 85284 060 9 160pp £7.99

TOUR OF MONT BLANC *Andrew Harper* One of the world's best walks - the circumnavigation of the Mont Blanc massif. ISBN 1 85284 240 7 168pp PVC cover

TOUR OF THE OISANS: GR54 *Andrew Harper* Around the massif, similar in quality to the Tour of Mont Blanc. ISBN 1 85284 157 5 120pp PVC cover £9.99

THE TOUR OF THE QUEYRAS *Alan Castle* 13 days across the sunniest part of the French Alps. Suitable for a first Alpine visit. ISBN 1 85284 048 X 160pp £6.99

TOUR OF THE VANOISE *Kev Reynolds* A circuit of one of the finest mountain areas of France. The second most popular mountain tour after the Tour of Mont Blanc. ISBN

1 85284 224 5 120pp £7.99

WALKING THE FRENCH ALPS: GR5 *Martin Collins* The popular From Lake Geneva to Nice. Split into stages, each of which could form the basis of a good holiday. ISBN 1 85284 051 X 160pp £8.99

WALKING THE FRENCH GORGES *Alan Castle* 320 miles through Provence and Ardèche, includes the famous Verdon. ISBN 1 85284 114 1 224pp £7.99

WALKING IN THE TARENTAISE & BEAUFORTAIN ALPS *J.W. Akitt* Delectable mountains south of Mont Blanc includes the Vanoise National Park. 53 day walks, 5 tours between 2 and 8 days duration, plus 40 short outings. ISBN 1 85284 181 8 216pp £9.99

WALKS IN VOLCANO COUNTRY *Alan Castle* Two LD walks in Central France- the High Auvergne and Tour of the Velay - in a unique landscape of extinct volcanoes. ISBN 1 85284 092 7 208pp £8.50

THE WAY OF ST JAMES: GR65 *H.Bishop* French section of the pilgrim's route, across Massif Central from Le Puy to the Pyrenees. ISBN 1 85284 029 3 96pp £5.50

FRANCE/SPAIN

WALKS & CLIMBS IN THE PYRENEES *Kev Reynolds* Includes the Pyrenean High Level Route.. (3rd Edition) ISBN 1 85284 133 8 328pp PVC cover £14.99

SPAIN

WALKING IN MALLORCA *June Parker.* The 3rd edition takes account of rapidly changing conditions. Includes the classic multi-day walk through the backbone of the mountains. One of the great walking guides. ISBN 1 85284 250 4

THE MOUNTAINS OF CENTRAL SPAIN *Jaqueline Oglesby* Walks and scrambles in the Sierras de Gredos and Guadarrama which rise to 2600m and are snow capped for five months of the year. ISBN 1 85284 203 2 312p £14.99

THROUGH THE SPANISH PYRENEES: GR11 *Paul Lucia* A new long distance trail which mirrors the French GR10 but traverses much lonelier, wilder country ISBN 1 85284 222 9 216pp £10.99

WALKING IN THE SIERRA NEVADA *Andy Walmsley* Spain's highest mountain range, a wonderland for traveller and wilderness backpacker. Mountain bike routes are indicated. ISBN 1 85284 194 X 160pp £8.99

THE WAY OF ST JAMES: SPAIN *Alison Raju* The popular Pilgrim Road from the Pyrenees to Santiago de Compostela. ISBN 1 85284 142 7 152pp £7.99

SWITZERLAND including adjacent parts of France and Italy

ALPINE PASS ROUTE, SWITZERLAND *Kev Reynolds* Over 15 passes along the northern edge of the Alps, past the Eiger, Jungfrau and many other renowned peaks. ISBN 1 85284 069 2 176pp £6.99

CHAMONIX to ZERMATT The Walker's Haute Route *Kev Reynolds* In the shadow of great peaks from Mont Blanc to the Matterhorn. ISBN 1 85284 215 6 176pp £7.99

THE JURA: WALKING THE HIGH ROUTE *Kev Reynolds* **WINTER SKI TRAVERSES** *R.Brian Evans* The High

Route is a LD path along the highest crest of the Swiss Jura. In winter the area is a paradise for cross-country skiers. *ISBN 1 85284 010 2 192pp £6.99*

THE GRAND TOUR OF MONTE ROSA *C.J.Wright*
Vol 1 - Martigny to Valle della Sesia (via the Italian valleys) *ISBN 1 85284 177 X 216pp £14.99*
Vol 2 - Valle della Sesia to Martigny (via the Swiss valleys) *ISBN 1 85284 178 8 182pp £14.99* The ultimate alpine LD walk which encircles most of the Pennine Alps.

GERMANY, AUSTRIA & EASTERN EUROPE
GERMANY'S ROMANTIC ROAD A guide for walkers and cyclists *Gordon McLachlan* 423km past historic walled towns and castles of southern Germany . *ISBN 1 85284 233 4 208pp £9.99 (May)*

HUT TO HUT IN THE STUBAI ALPS *Allan Hartley* Two classic tours: The Stubai Rucksack Route and The Stubai Glacier Tour, each taking around 10 days. Easy peaks and good huts make it a good area for a first Alpine season. *ISBN 1 85284 123 0 128pp Card cover £6.99*

KING LUDWIG WAY *Fleur and Colin Speakman* Travels the Bavarian countryside from Munich to Füssen. King Ludwig was responsible for the fabulous castle of Neuschwanstein . *ISBN 0 902363 90 5 80pp £3.99*

MOUNTAIN WALKING IN AUSTRIA *Cecil Davies* Describes walks in 17 mountain groups, from single day to multi-day hut to hut excursions. *ISBN 1 85284 239 3 200pp*

WALKING IN THE BLACK FOREST *Fleur & Colin Speakman* Above the Rhine valley, the Westweg was Europe's first waymarked trail in 1900. *ISBN 1 85284 050 1 120pp £5.99*

SCANDINAVIA
WALKING IN NORWAY *Connie Roos* 20 walking routes in the main mountain areas from the far south to the sub arctic regions, all accessible by public transport. *ISBN 1 85284 230 X 200pp £10.99*

ITALY & SLOVENIA
ALTA VIA - HIGH LEVEL WALKS IN THE DOLOMITES *Martin Collins* A guide to some of the most popular mountain paths in Europe - Alta Via 1 and 2. *ISBN 0 902363 75 1 160pp PVC cover £8.99*

THE GRAND TOUR OF MONTE ROSA *C.J.Wright* See entry under Switzerland

LONG DISTANCE WALKS IN THE GRAN PARADISO *J.W. Akitt.* Describes Alta Via 2 and the Grand Traverse of Gran Paradiso.. *ISBN 1 85284 247 4*

MEDITERRANEAN COUNTRIES
THE ATLAS MOUNTAINS *Karl Smith* Trekking in the mountains of north Africa. Practical and comprehensive. *ISBN 1 85284 032 3 136pp PVC cover £9.99*

CRETE OFF THE BEATEN TRACK *Bruce and Naomi Caughey* Short walks, mountain hikes, gorges, coves and beaches. Ruins of ancient civilizations abound. *ISBN 1 85284 019 6 152pp £7.99*

THE MOUNTAINS OF GREECE. A Walker's Guide *Tim Salmon* Hikes of all grades from a month-long traverse of

the Pindos to day hikes on the outskirts of Athens. *ISBN 1 85284 108 7 PVC cover £9.99*

THE MOUNTAINS OF TURKEY *Karl Smith* Over 100 treks and scrambles with detailed descriptions of all the popular peaks. Includes Ararat. *ISBN 1 85284 161 3 184pp PVC cover £14.99*

TREKS AND CLIMBS in WADI RUM, JORDAN *Tony Howard.* The world's foremost desert climbing and trekking area.*ISBN 1 85284 135 4 252pp A5 Card cover £12.99*

THE ALA DAG, Climbs and Treks in Turkey's Crimson Mountains *O.B.Tüzel* The best mountaineering area in Turkey. *ISBN 1 85284 112 5 296pp PVC cover £14.99*

HIMALAYA
ANNAPURNA - A Trekker's Guide *Kev Reynolds* Includes Annapurna Circuit, Annapurna Sanctuary and Pilgrim's Trail, with lots of good advice. *ISBN 1 85284 132 X 184p £8.99*

EVEREST - A Trekker's Guide *Kev Reynolds* The most popular trekking region in the Himalaya. Lodges, teahouse, permits, health - all are dealt with in this indispensible guide. *ISBN 1 85284 187 7 £8.99*

LANGTANG, GOSAINKUND & HELAMBU - A Trekker's Guide *Kev Reynolds* Popular area, easily accessible from Kathmandu. *ISBN 1 85284 207 5 £8.99*

ADVENTURE TREKS IN NEPAL *Bill O'Connor* *ISBN 1 85223 306 0 160pp large format £9.99*

OTHER COUNTRIES
MOUNTAIN WALKING IN AFRICA 1: KENYA *David Else* Detailed route descriptions and practical information. *ISBN 1 85365 205 9 180pp A5 size £9.99*

TREKKING IN THE CAUCAUSUS *Yuri Kolomiets & Aleksey Solovyev* Hidden until recently behind the Iron Curtain. Included are the highest tops in Europe, the summits of Mt Elbrus. *ISBN 1 85284 129 X 224pp PVC cover £14.99*

ADVENTURE TREKS WESTERN NORTH AMERICA *Chris Townsend ISBN 1 85223 317 6 160pp large format £9.99*

CLASSIC TRAMPS IN NEW ZEALAND *Constance Roos* The 14 best long distance walks in both South and North Islands. *ISBN 1 85284 118 4 208pp PVC cover £14.99*